The Language of
Fashion Illustration

The Language of Fashion Illustration

THE LANGUAGE OF FASHION ILLUSTRATION
Copyright © 2008 by **maomao** publications

Published and distributed in Europe by:
Index Book, S.L.
Consell de Cent, 160, local 3
08015 Barcelona
Tel.: +34 93 454 55 47 Fax: +34 93 454 84 38
E-mail: ib@indexbook.com/www.indexbook.com

Drawings y texts: Maite Lafuente
Copy-editing: Peter Ridding
Layout: Emma Termes

ISBN-13: 978-84-96774-60-5

Printed in Spain

All rights reserved. No part of this publication may be reproduced or transmitted in any form or by any means, electronic or mechanical, including photocopy, recording or any information storage and retrieval system, without permission in writing from the copyright owner(s).

The captions and artwork in this book are based on material supplied by the designers whose work is included. While every effort has been made to ensure their accuracy, **maomao** does under any circumstances accept any responsibility for any error or omissions.

- 6 Introduction
- 10 Shirts, sweaters
- 34 Skirts, dresses, trousers
- 66 Jackets, coats
- 84 Underwear, swimwear, sportswear
- 114 Accessories
- 146 Details
- 170 Patterns

Drawing plays a primordial role in all creative fields, and it is all the more important when one works with a team of people. In any given fashion company, be it small or large, one can be sure that from conception to manufacture, the designs will go through many—at times over a dozen— pairs of hands.

Ever so often, magazines reveal a couple of pages from famous designers' sketchbooks to the general public. Usually these pages look like a patchwork of sample materials, colourful, elegant lines, and text more closely resembling graffiti than the formatted style taught in design school. This type of drawing is essential to the creative process because it is unique to the designer and it allows for his or her ideas to flow freely. The next step, however, consists in translating this vision to collaborators in a clear and precise manner. It is at this point that fashion illustration as it is demonstrated in this book comes into play. These illustrations may seem a little flat, or lacking in personality, but in focusing on the technical details, they bridge the gap between the abstract and the concrete, allowing one to go from the idea to the object.

Jackets, trousers, skirts, dresses, undergarments; accessories such as hats, shoes, gloves; details such as buttons, fastening systems, belts... One of the first lessons we learn is that style is in the details. We present here, through a very comprehensive list of elements that define a "look", the basics of a language common to the entire fashion industry.

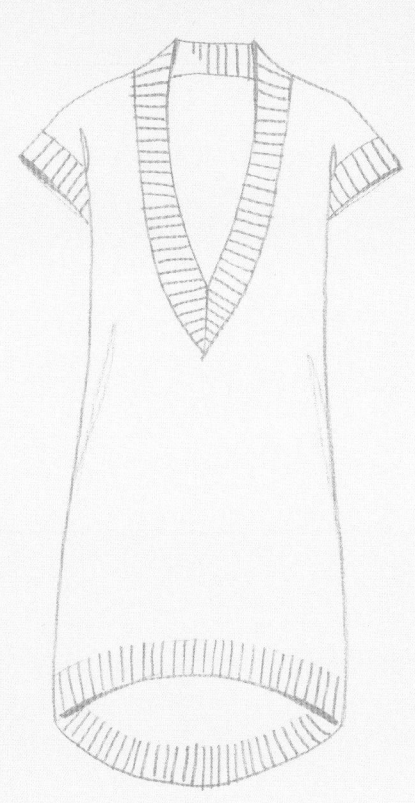

Shirts, sweaters

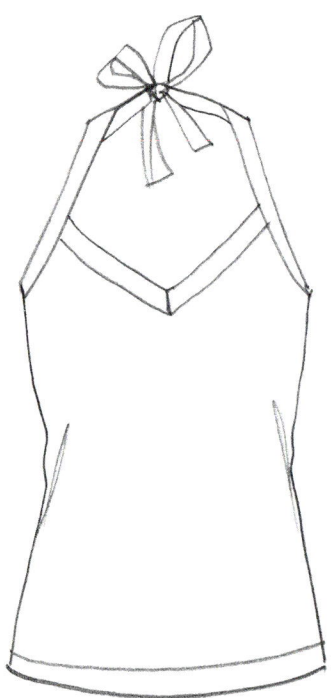

T-shirt tied around the neck

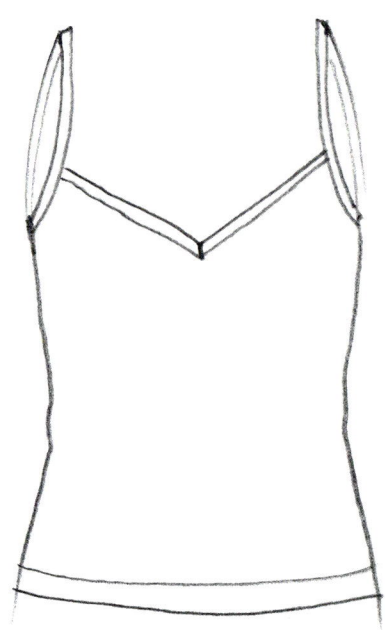

Straps T-shirt

Shirts, sweaters

T-shirt with square neckline and double fabric

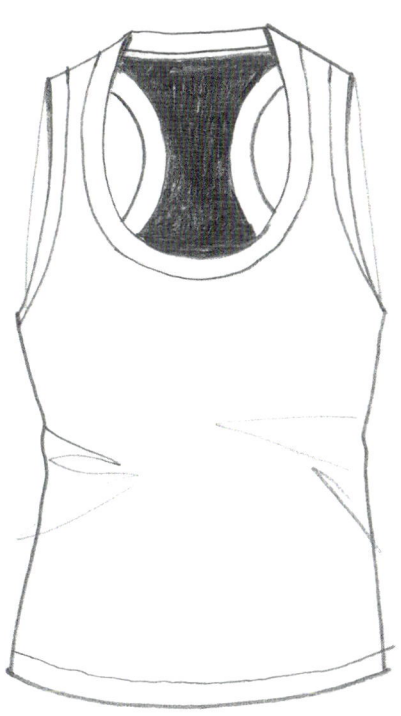

Two-color sports T-shirt with swimming back

Shirts, sweaters

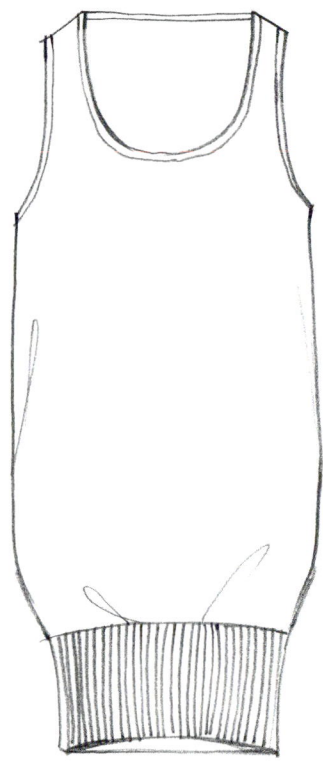
Sweater-dress

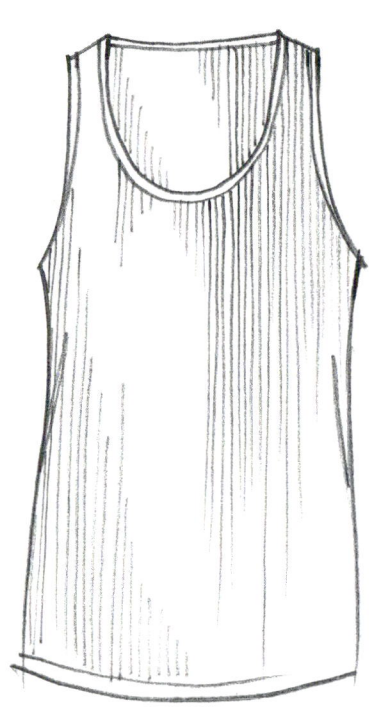
Tank top

Shirts, sweaters

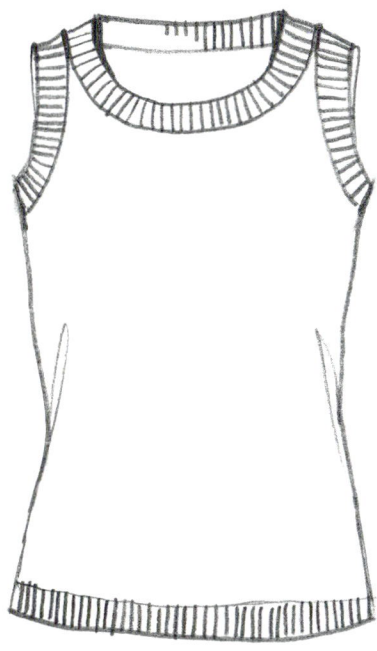

Sleeveless T-shirt with round neckline

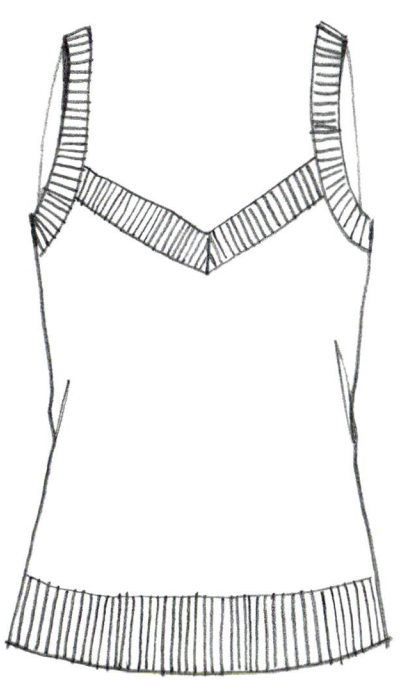

Straps T-shirt with peak neckline

Shirts, sweaters

Fitted T-shirt with crew neckline and short sleeves

Fitted T-shirt with loose V neckline and elbow sleeves

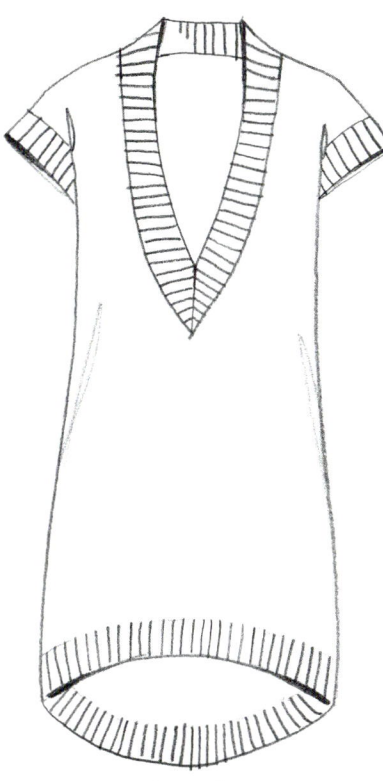

T-shirt dress

Cache-cœur

Shirts, sweaters

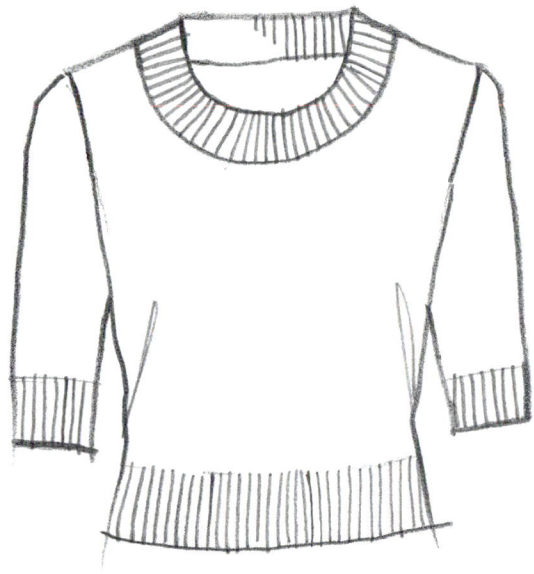

Sweater with crew neckline and elbow sleeves

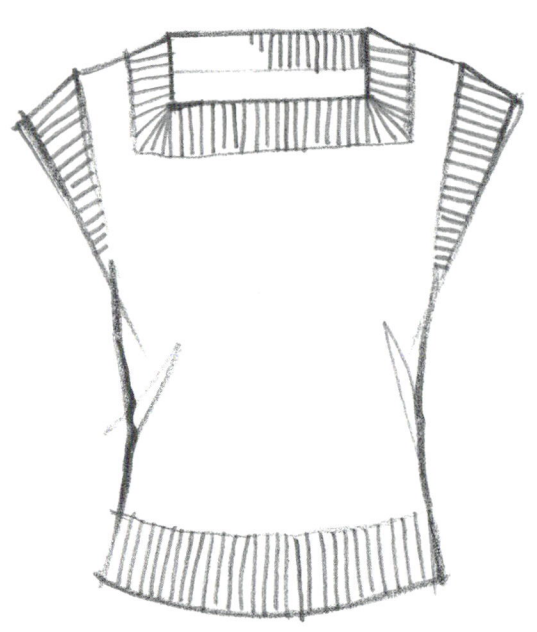

Sweater with square neckline

Shirts, sweaters

Sweatshirt without sleeves, fallen shoulders

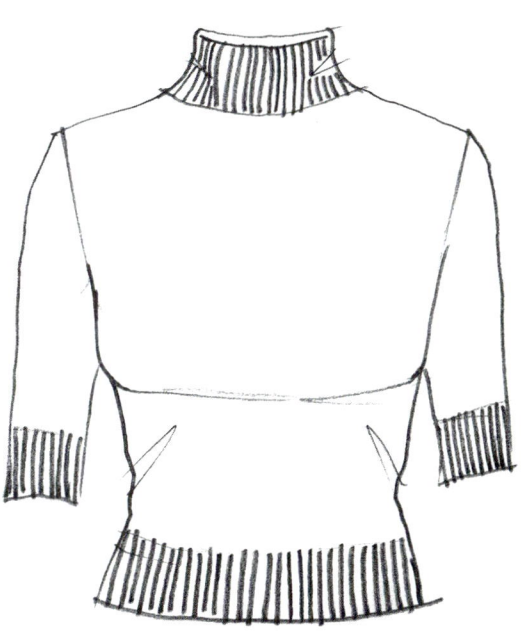

Sweater with semi-turtleneck

Shirts, sweaters

Shirts, sweaters

Polo shirt

Mini smocking neckline sweater with reverse stitch, rest plain and tubulars

Polo shirt with long facing and elbow sleeves

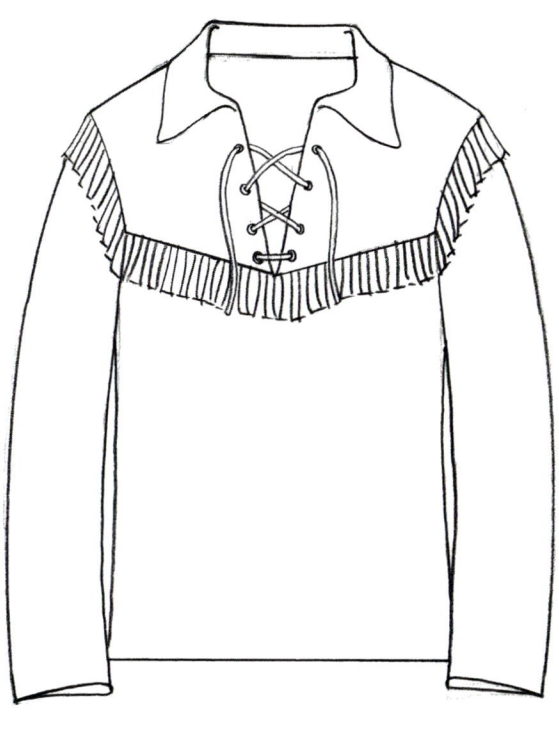

Cowboy shirt

Shirts, sweaters

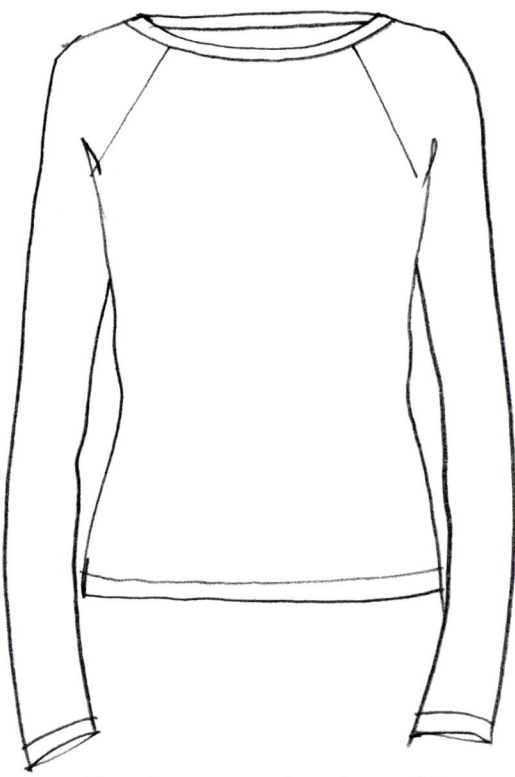

Closed scoop and raglan t-shirt

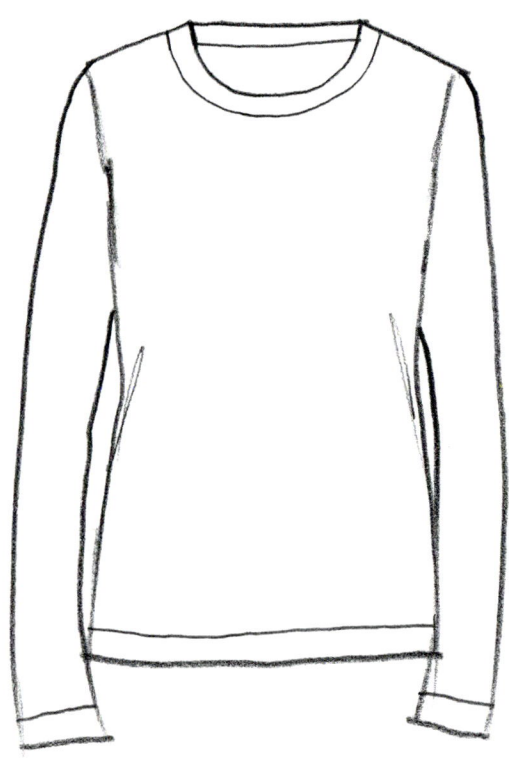

Loose fitting T-shirt with round neck and long sleeves

Low scoop neck and 3/4 length sleeve T-shirt

Round neck T-shirt with 3/4 length sleeves, raglan and detailed seams

Shirts, sweaters

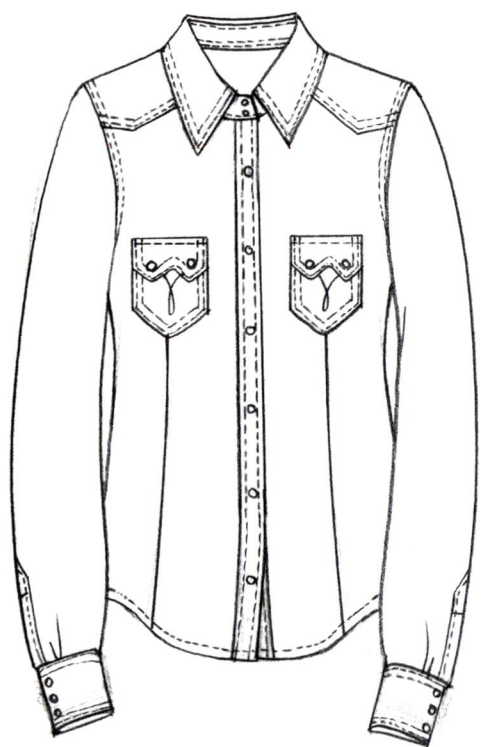

Denim shirt (front)

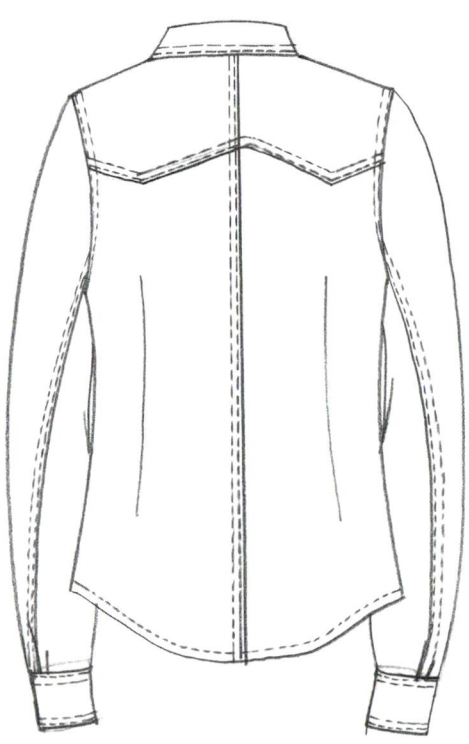

Denim shirt (back)

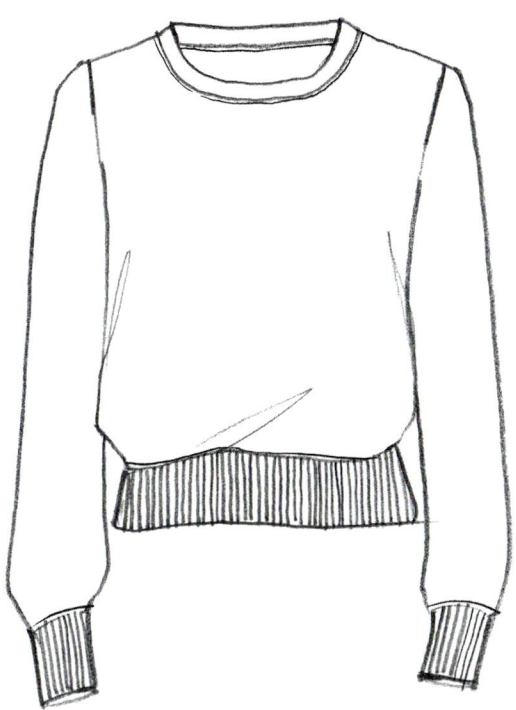

Plush T-shirt

Shirt with bow detail at the neck

Shirts, sweaters

Scoop neck top

Bat-wing sweater with 3/4 length sleeves and vertical stripes

Shirts, sweaters

Striped sweater with raglan and 3/4 length sleeves

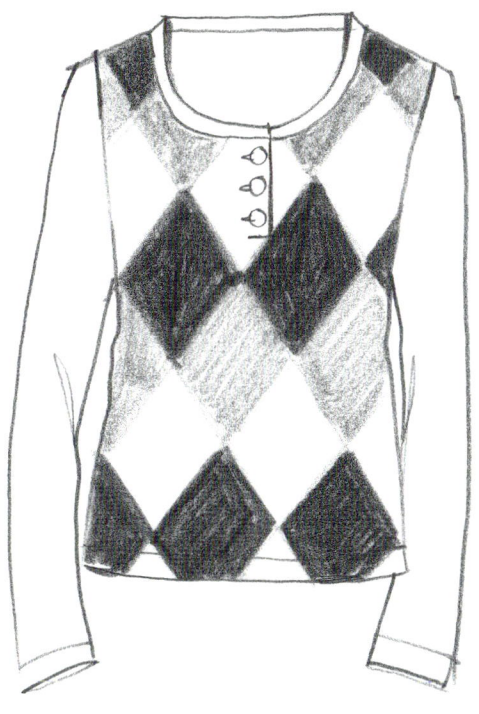

Intarsia sweater

Shirts, sweaters

Shirts, sweaters

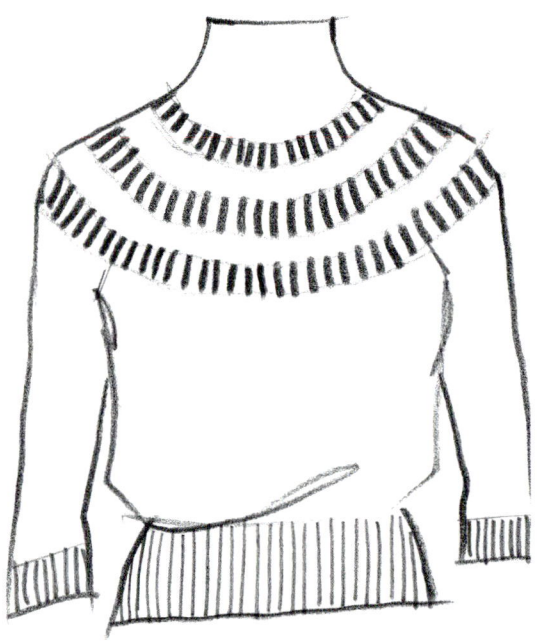

Sweater with braiding, 3/4 length sleeves and semi-turtleneck

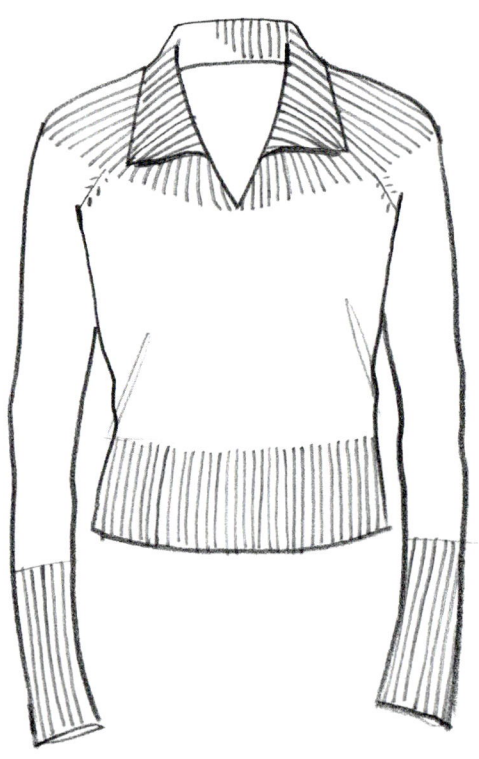

Shirt collar sweater ribbed at the top, on sleeves and bottom

Sweater with ribbed back, raglan and detailed seams

Sweater with incorporated scarf and 3/4 length sleeves

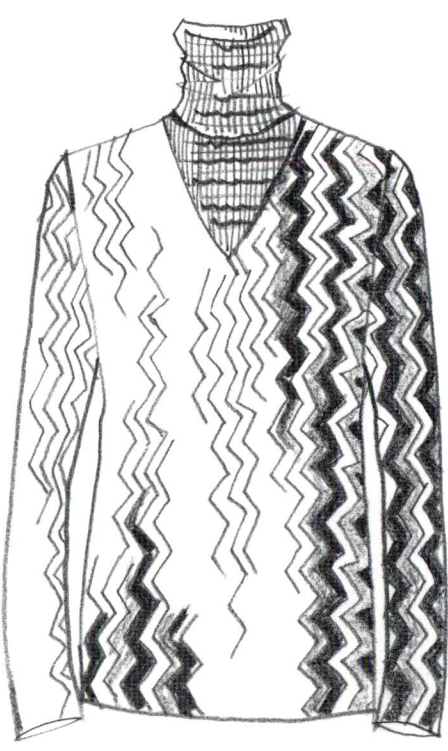

Multicolor zig-zag sweater

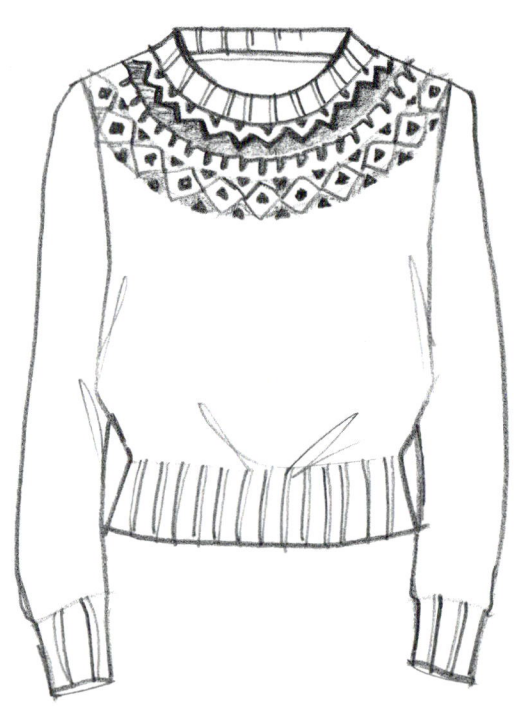

Fair Isle sweater

Shirts, sweaters

28

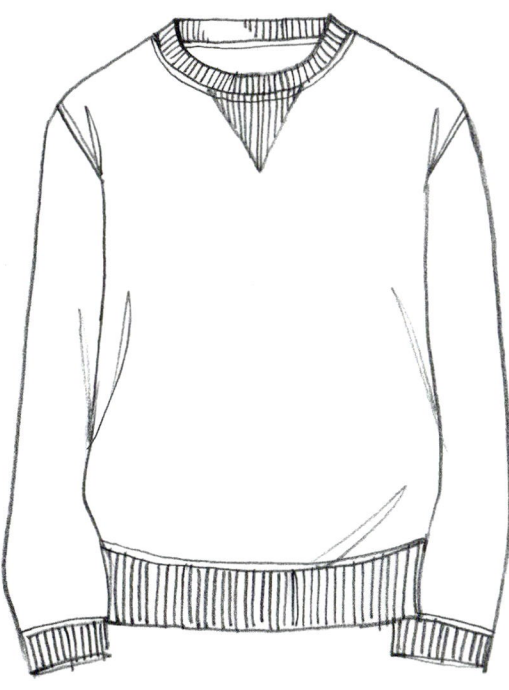

Basic sweater

Sweater with ribbed large neckline and pocket-belt

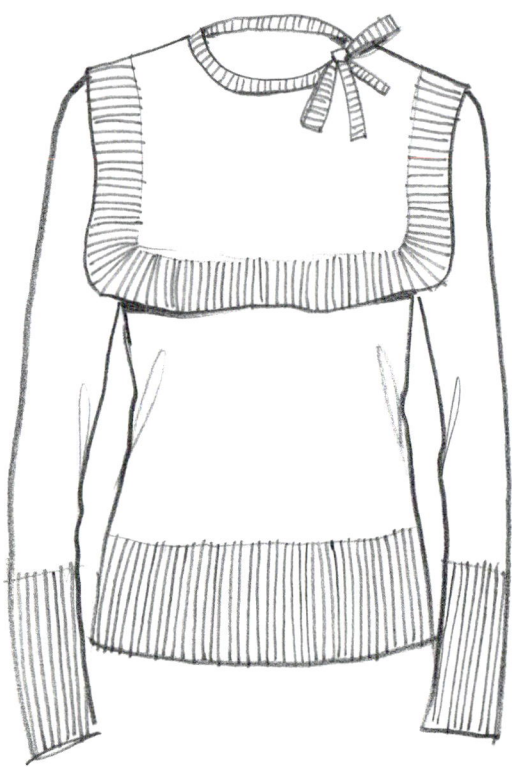

Capelet tubular sweater with bow

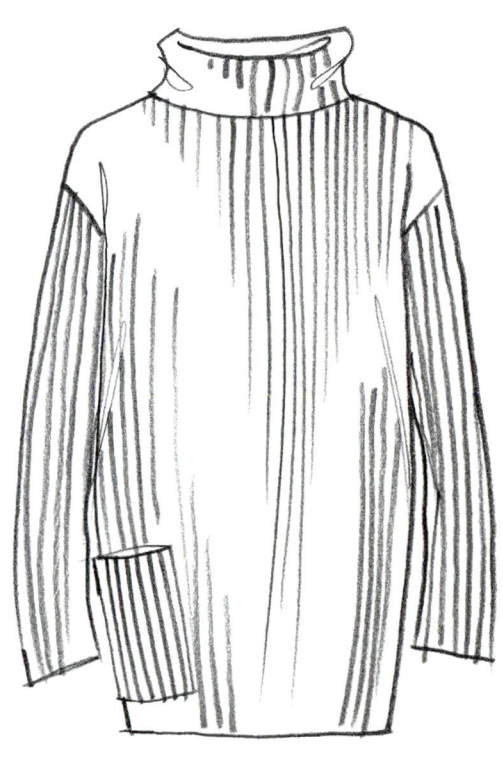

Full cardigan retro thick tunic with loose turtleneck

Shirts, sweaters

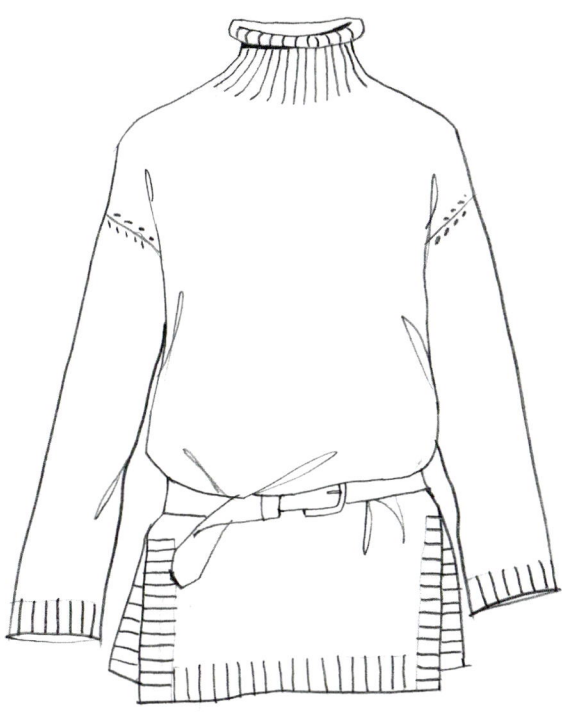

Belted tunic

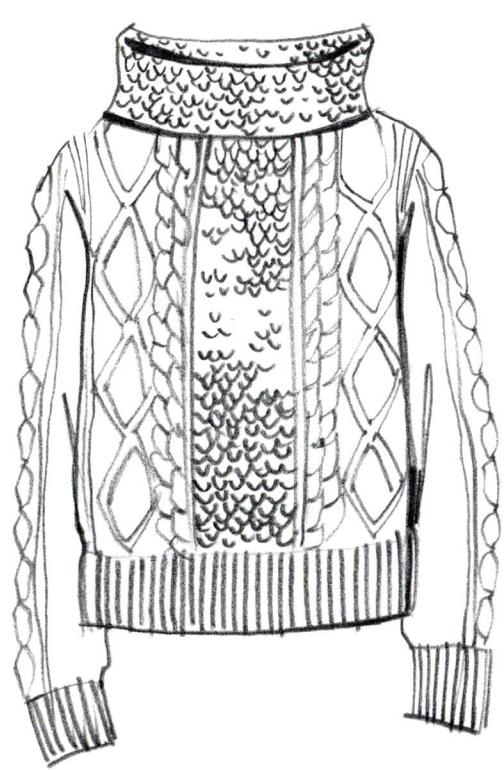

Thick Aran sweater with cable stitch and stretched turtleneck

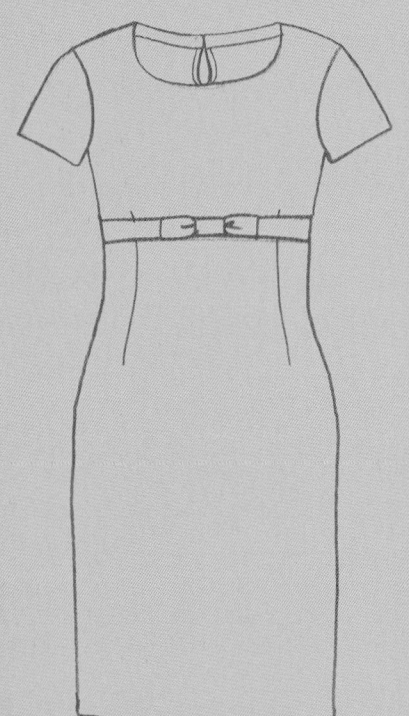

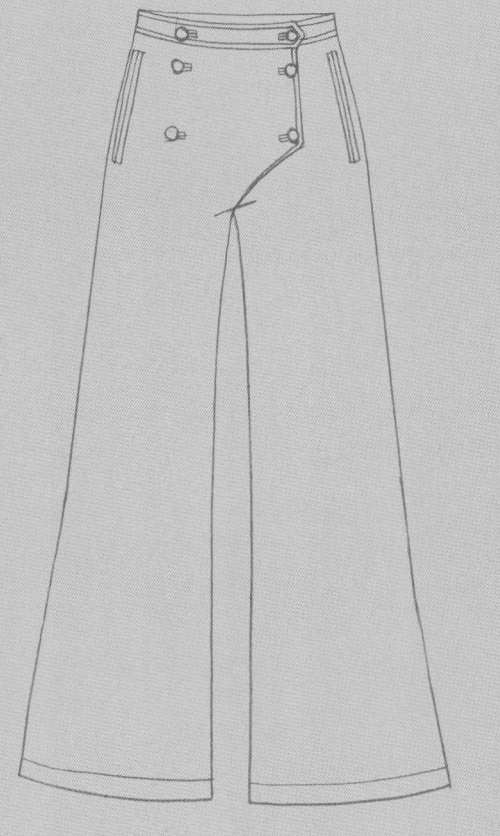

Skirts, dresses, trousers

Split skirt

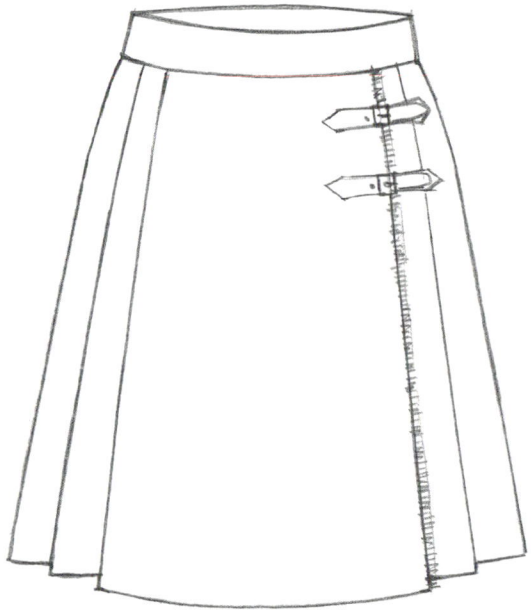

Scottish kilt

Pleated skirt

A-line skirt

Skirts, dresses, trousers

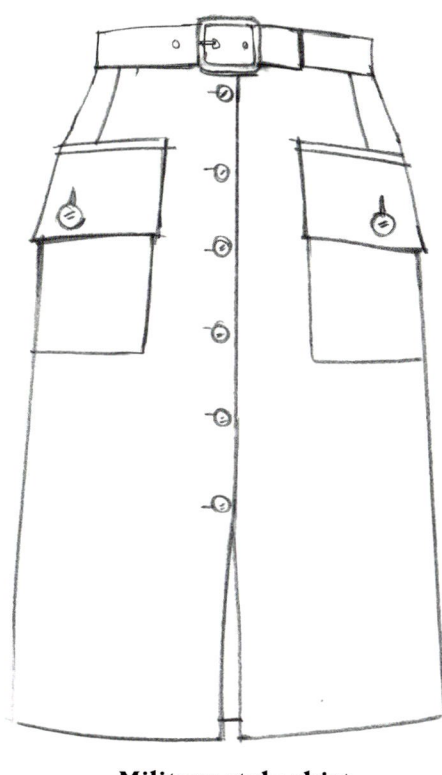

Military style skirt

Poof skirt

Tulip skirt

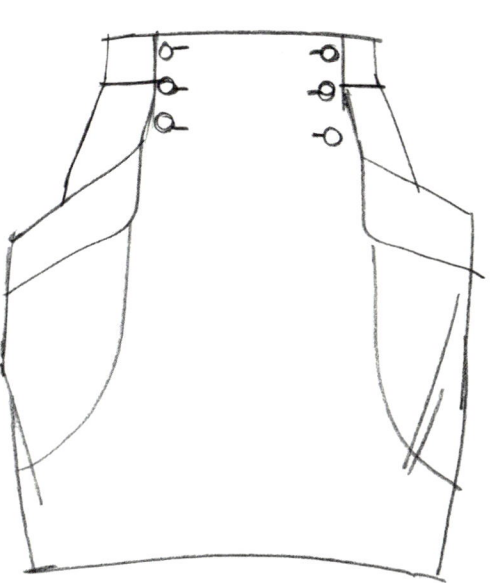

Sack skirt

Skirts, dresses, trousers

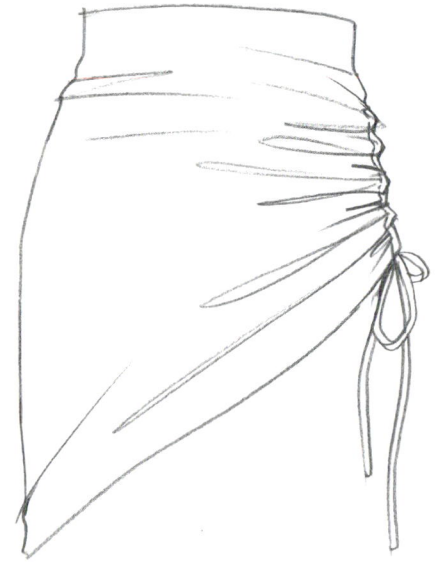

Straight skirt with side tuck **Balloon skirt**

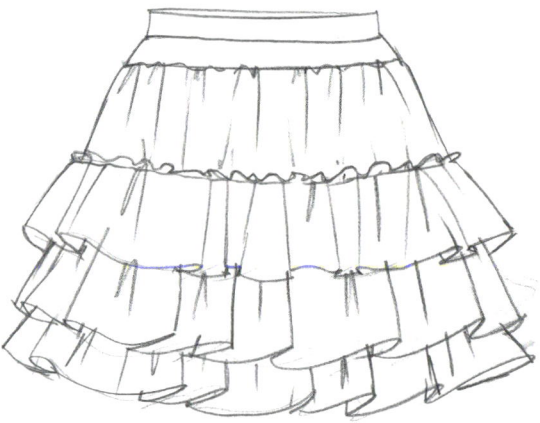

Ballerina skirt **Ruffle skirt**

Tie skirt

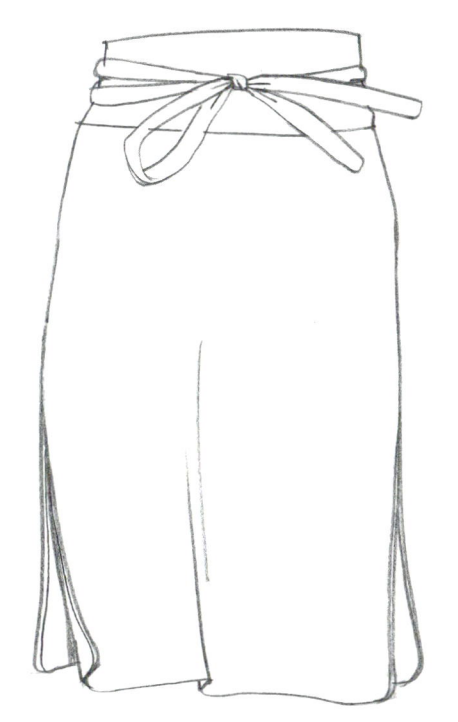

Skirt with side slits

Bubble skirt

Tulle cocktail skirt with ruffles

Skirts, dresses, trousers

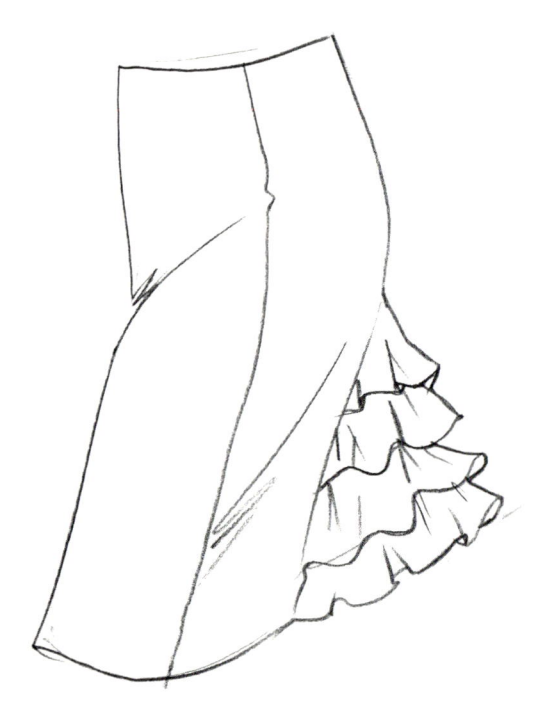

Skirt with ruffles on back (profile view)

Creased cocktail skirt

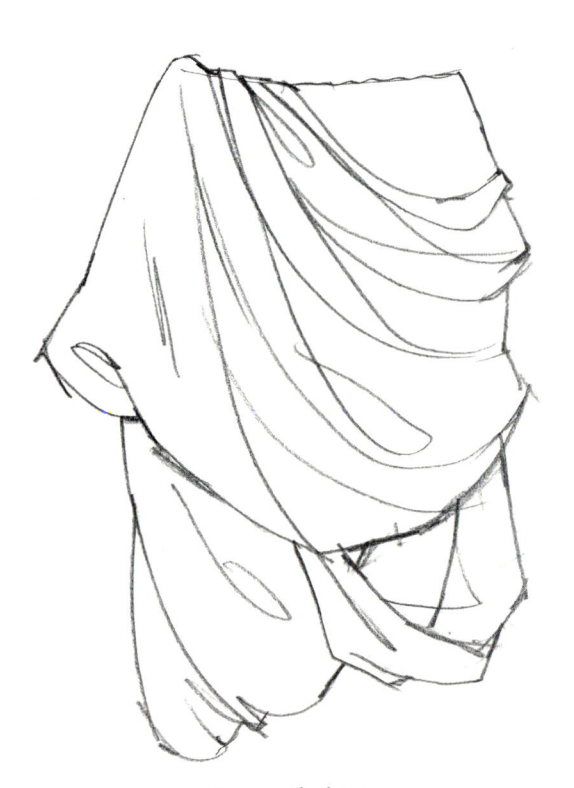

Draped skirt

Skirt

Skirts, dresses, trousers

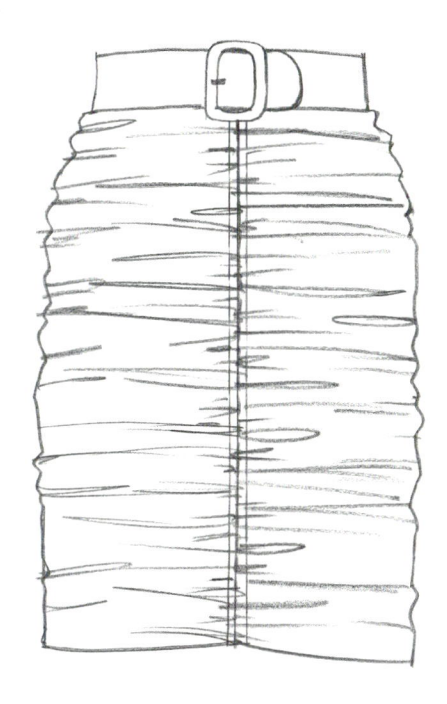

Creased skirt

Skirt with ruffles

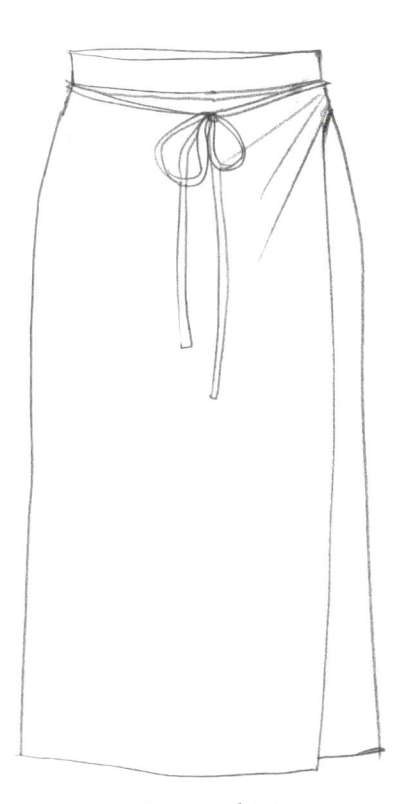

Apron skirt

Peasant skirt

Skirts, dresses, trousers

Skirts, dresses, trousers

Straight skirt

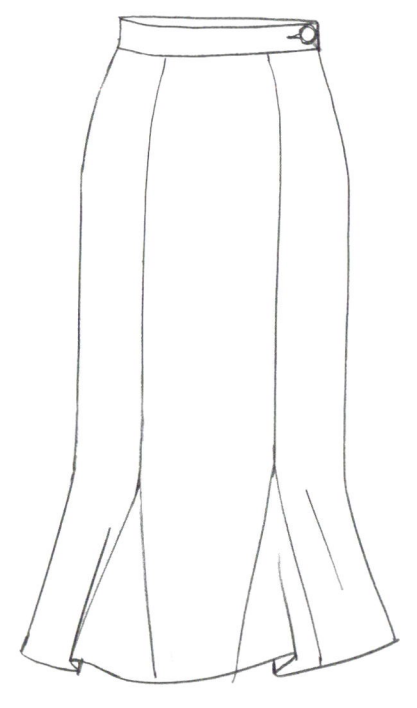

Godet skirt

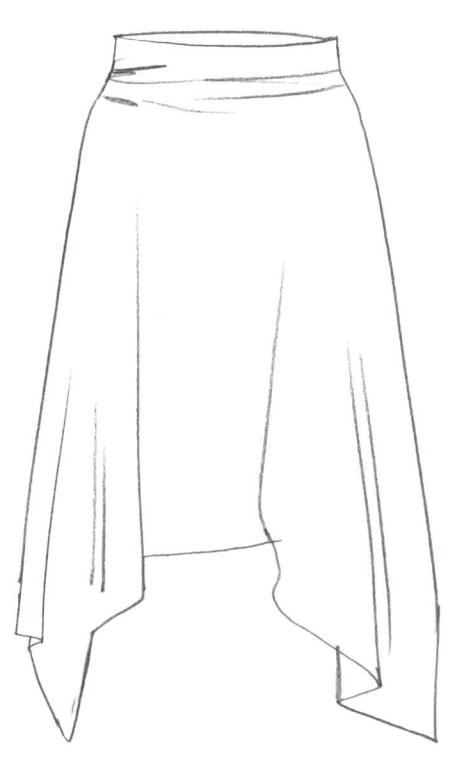

Handkerchief skirt

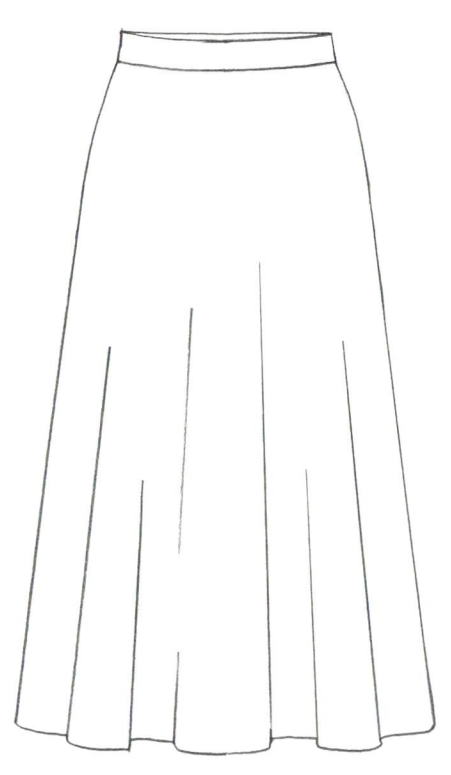

Layered skirt

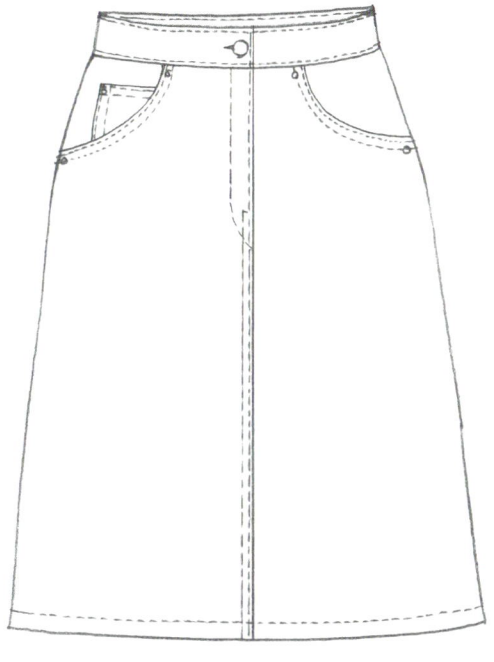

Denim skirt

Safari-style skirt

Can-can skirt with tutu

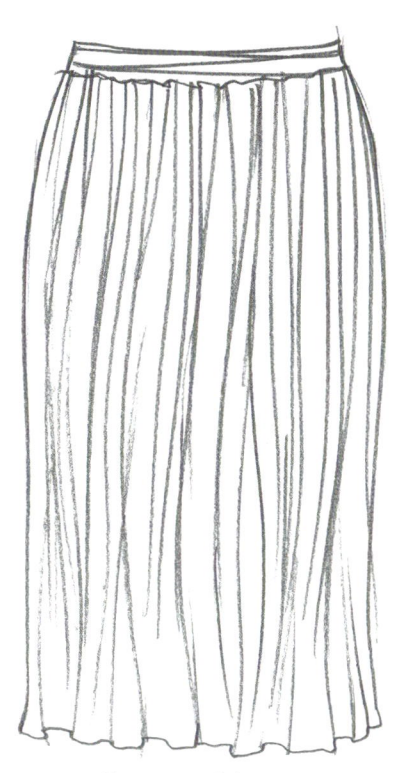

Fortuny skirt

Skirts, dresses, trousers

41

Mini dress with details in color contrast

Fine mini dress with glittering thread

Skirts, dresses, trousers

42

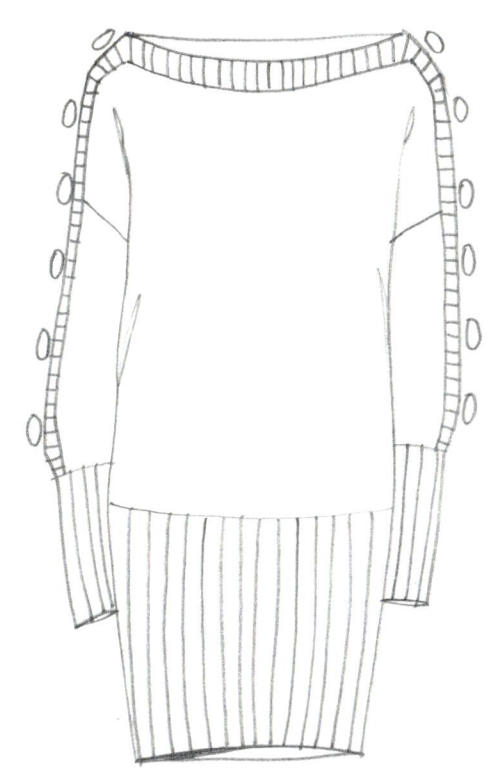

Tunic with wide ribbing, boat neckline and centre buttoning on sleeves

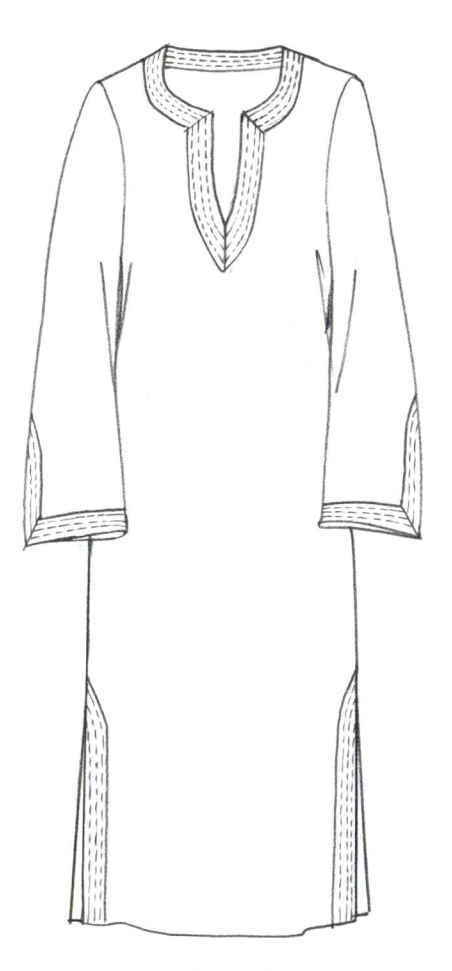

Djellaba-dress

Skirts, dresses, trousers

A-line dress

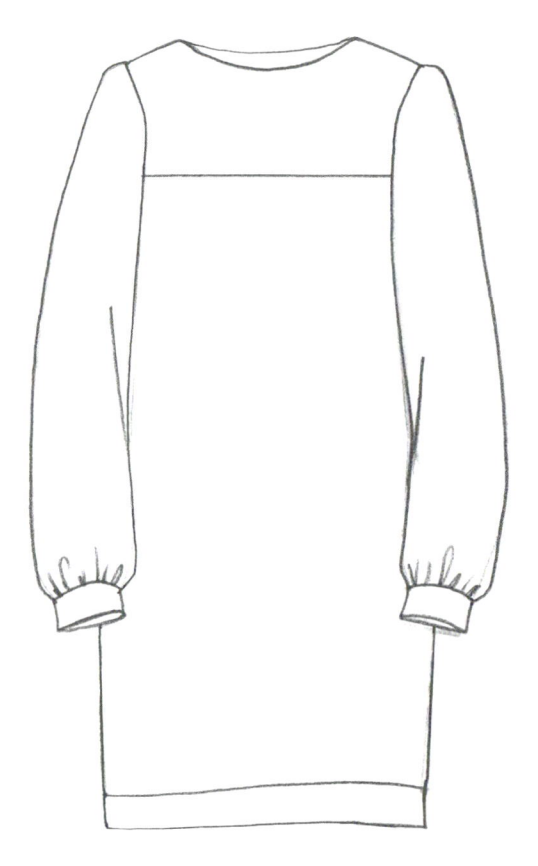

Sack dress

Skirts, dresses, trousers

Cocktail dress

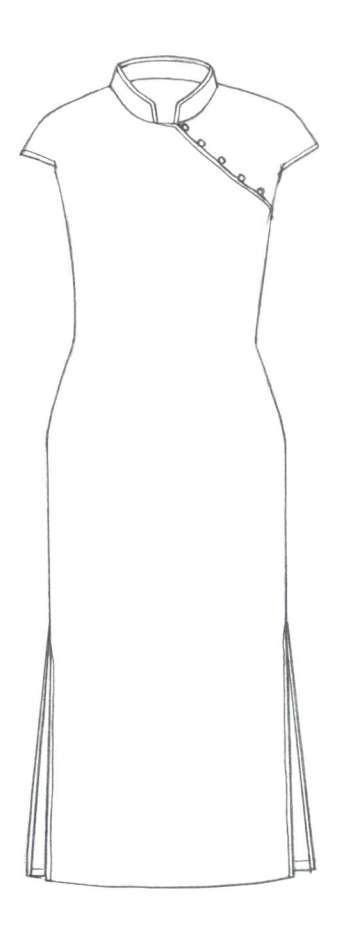

Chinese dress

Skirts, dresses, trousers

Retro 1950s dress

Halter neck dress

Skirts, dresses, trousers

Sabrina dress

Marilyn dress

Skirts, dresses, trousers

Fine halter-neck dress

Halter-neck with metal hoop dress

Skirts, dresses, trousers

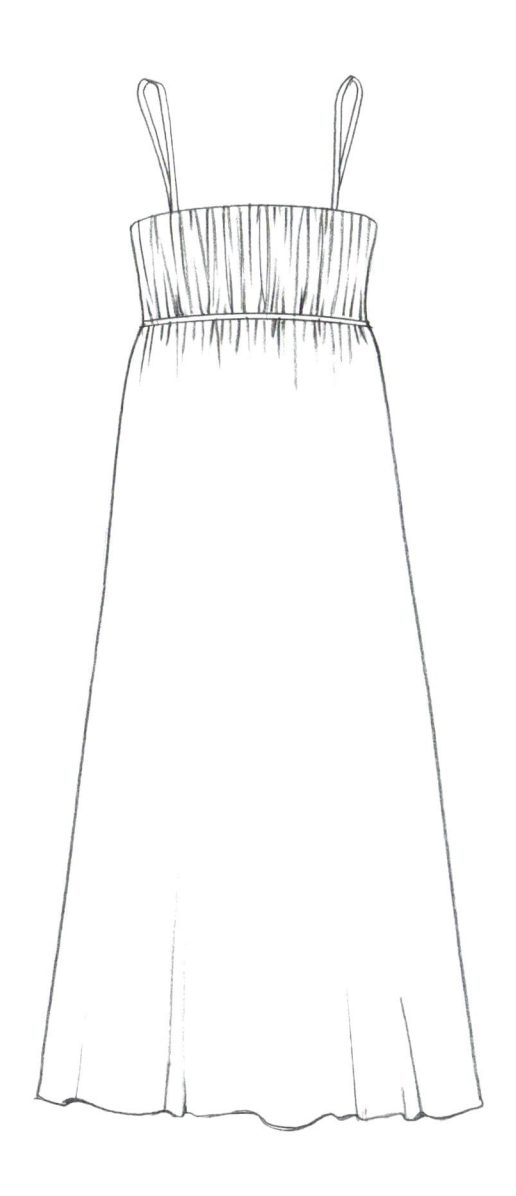

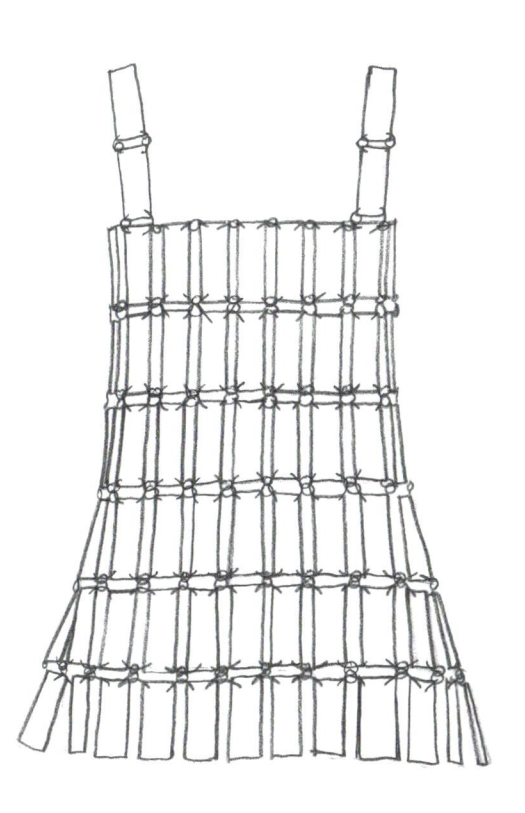

Empire dress

Paco Rabanne dress (with metal trim)

Skirts, dresses, trousers

Folk dress

One arm ruffled dress

Skirts, dresses, trousers

Draped nightdress

Gypsy dress

Skirts, dresses, trousers

51

Skirts, dresses, trousers

Princess line dress

Greek dress

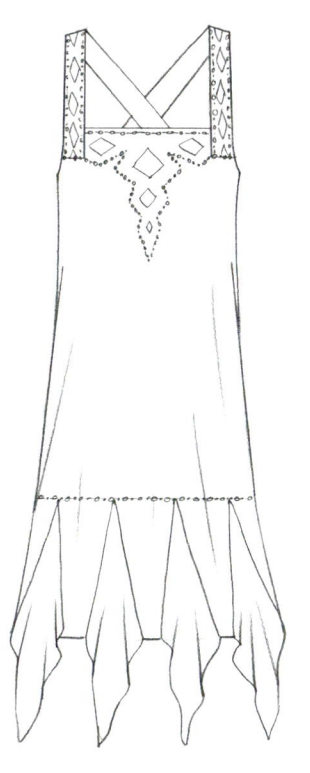

Charleston dress

Skirts, dresses, trousers

Skirts, dresses, trousers

Wide jeans

Baggy jeans

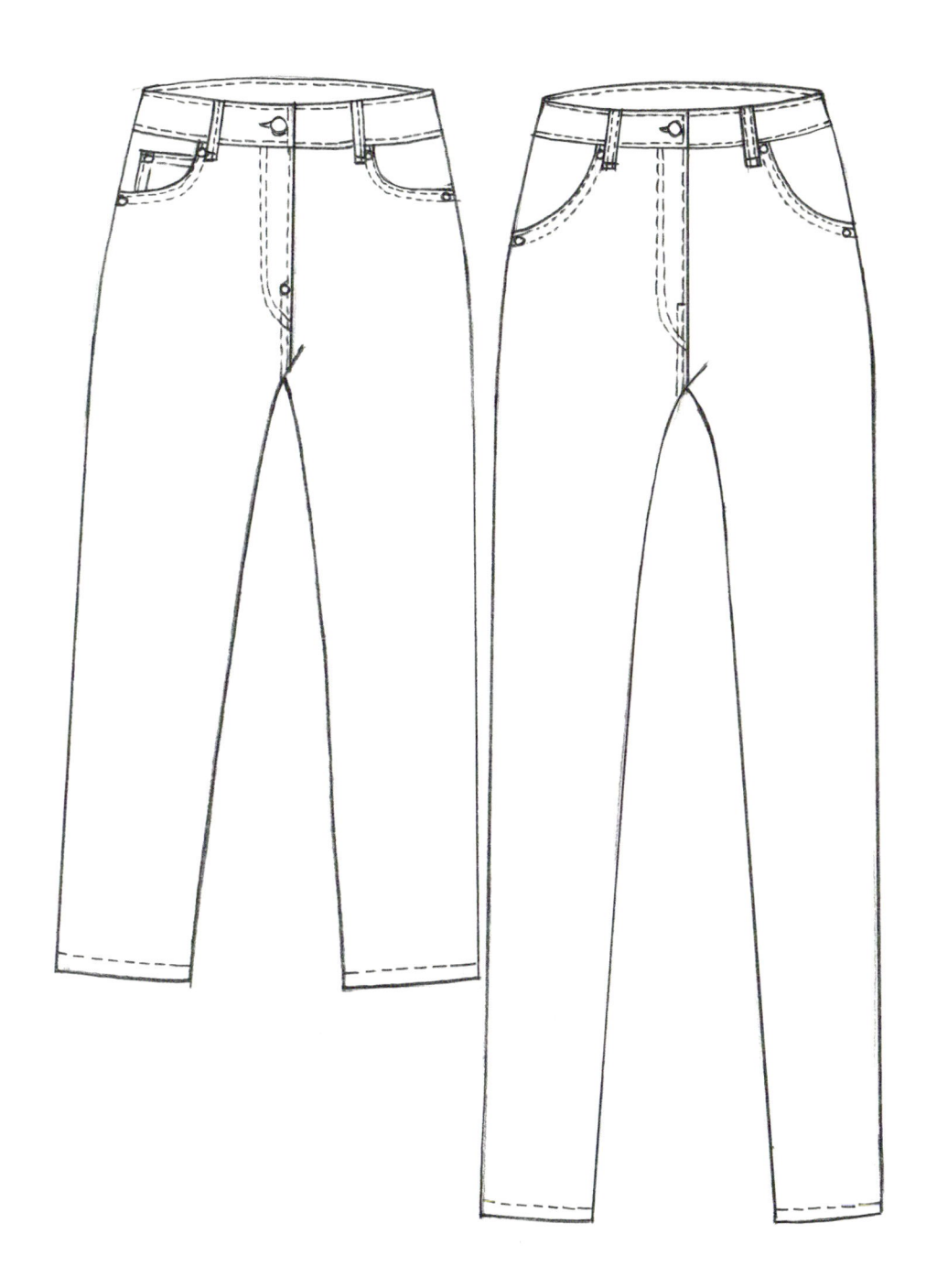

Capri jeans **Tight jeans**

Skirts, dresses, trousers

Skirts, dresses, trousers

Jodhpur pants   **Jodhpur pants (back)**

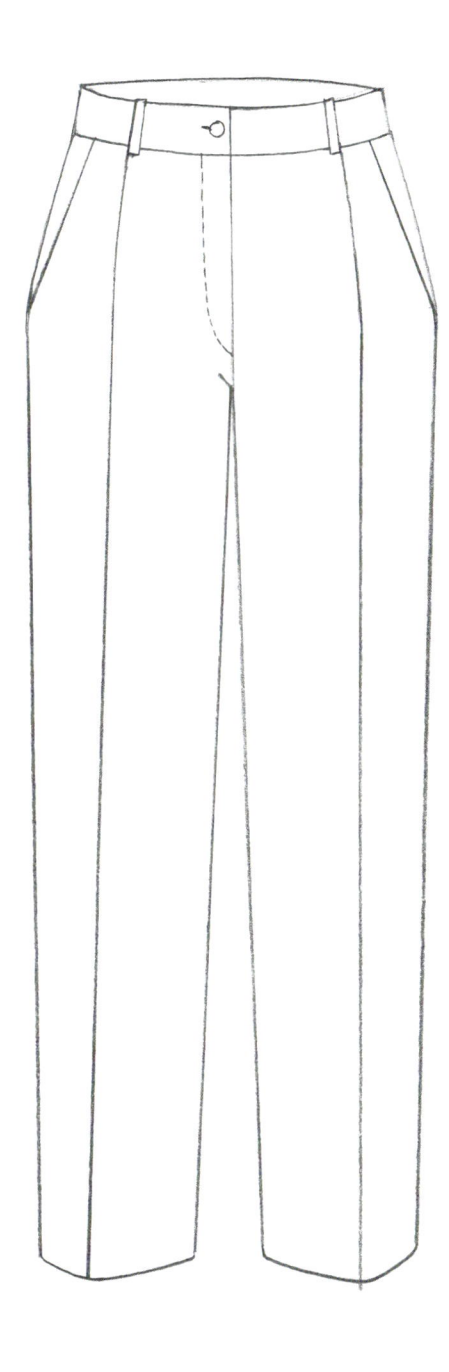

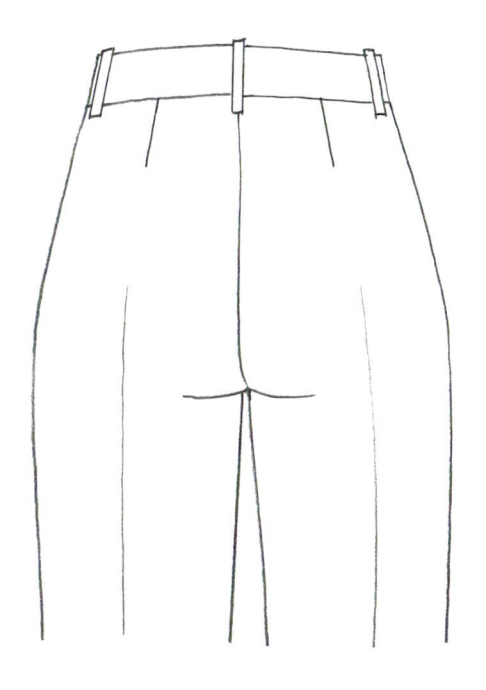

Classic pants   **Classic pants (back)**

Skirts, dresses, trousers

57

Leggings

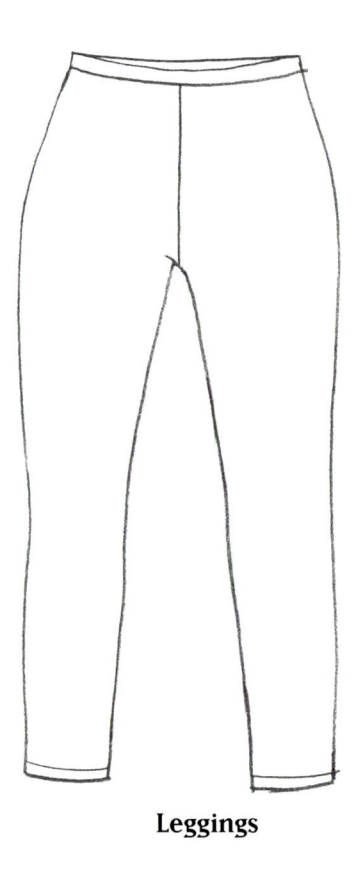

Cossack pants

Skirts, dresses, trousers

1980s Cossack pants

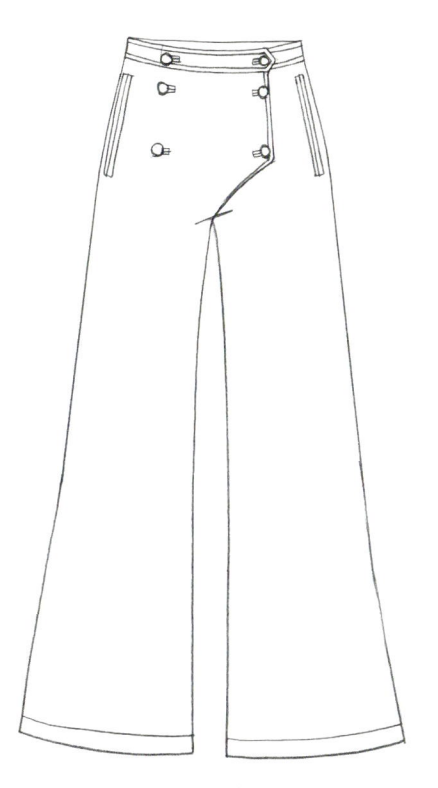

Marine-style pants

Skirts, dresses, trousers

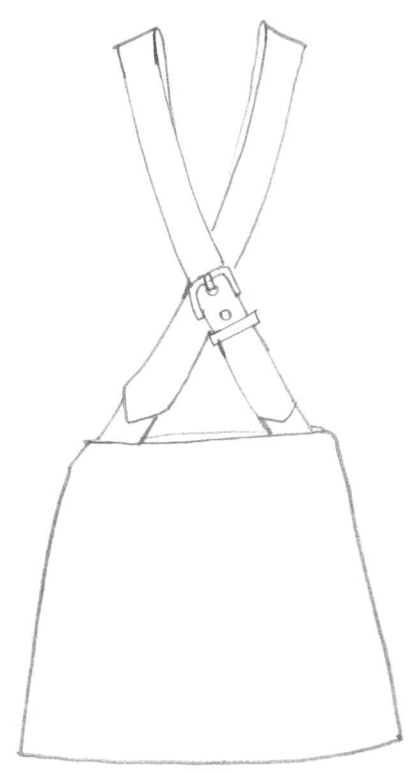

Mini skirt with compact stitch and crossed straps in front

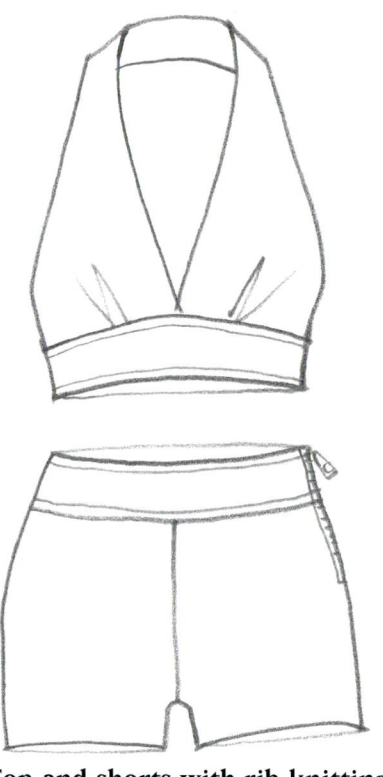

Top and shorts with rib knitting

Skirts, dresses, trousers

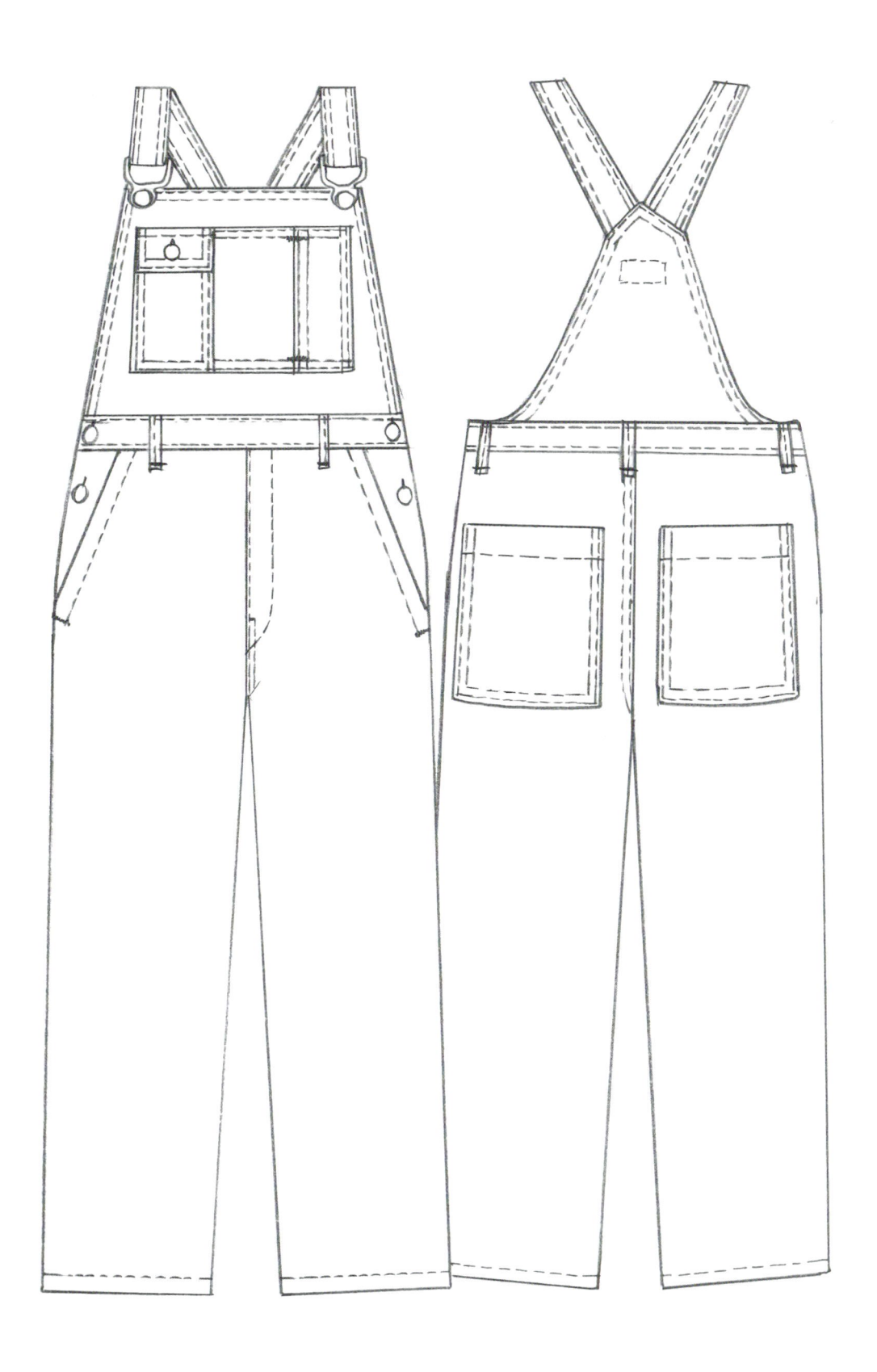

Denim overalls

Skirts, dresses, trousers

Shorts

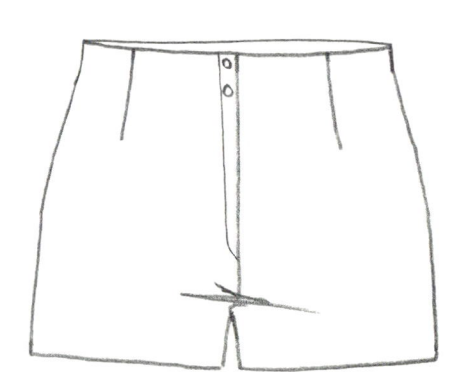

Poof shorts with bow

1960s style shorts

Skirts, dresses, trousers

Bermuda pants

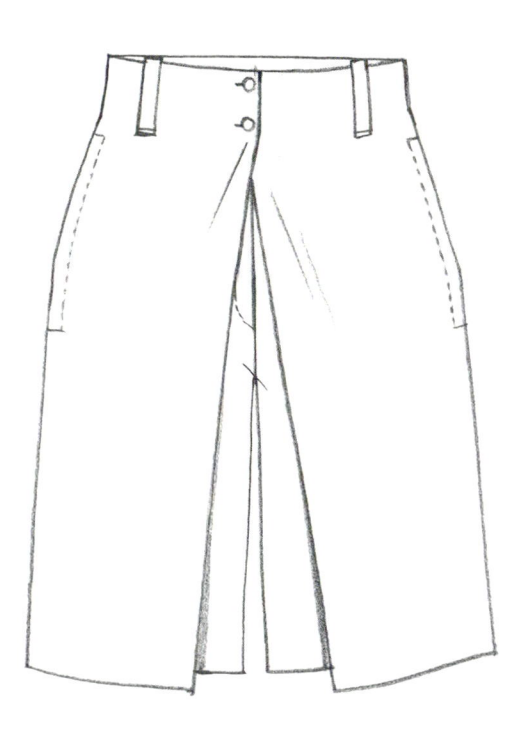

Apron pants

Skirts, dresses, trousers

63

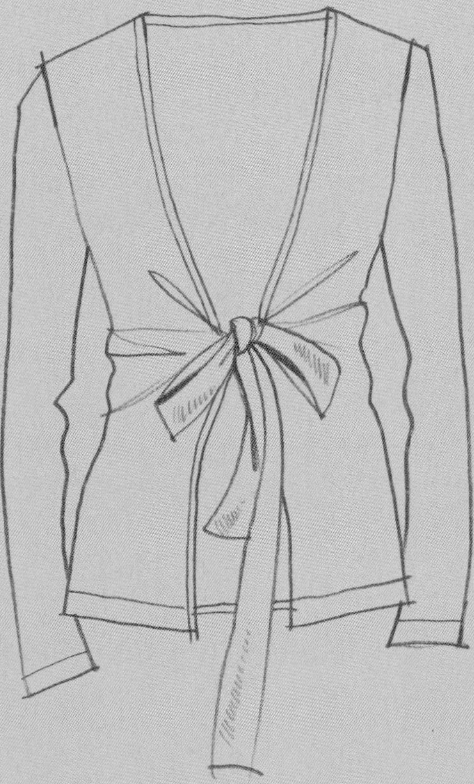

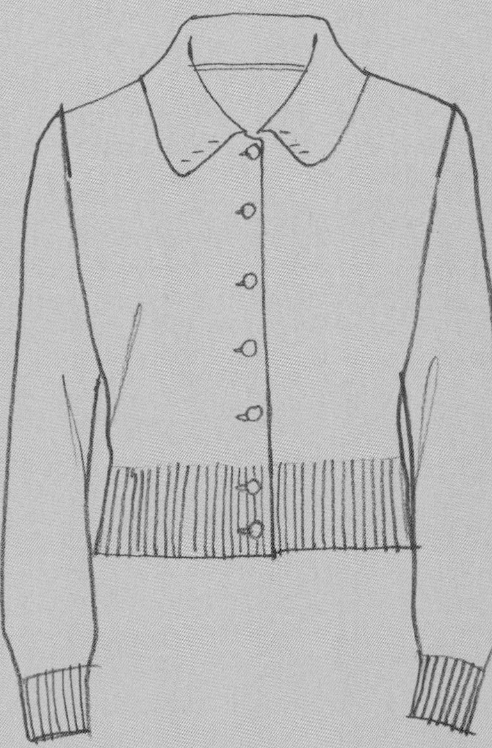

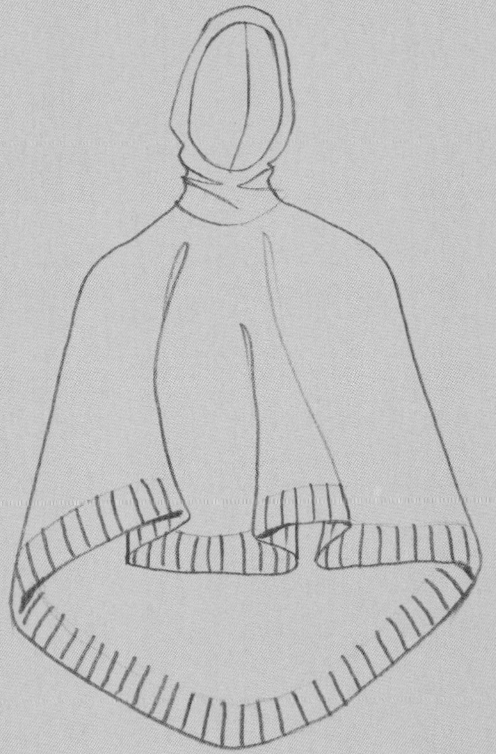

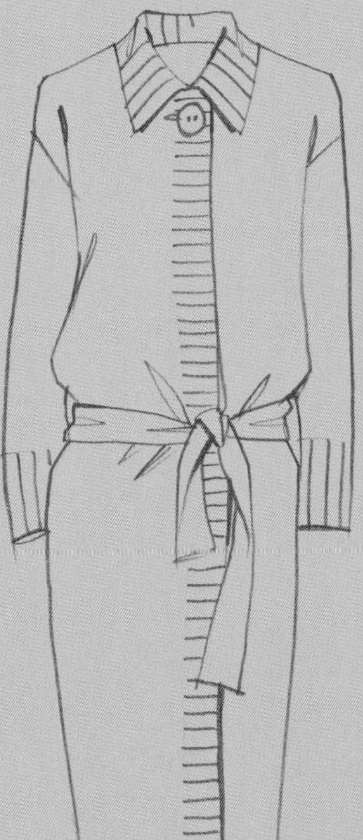

Jackets, coats

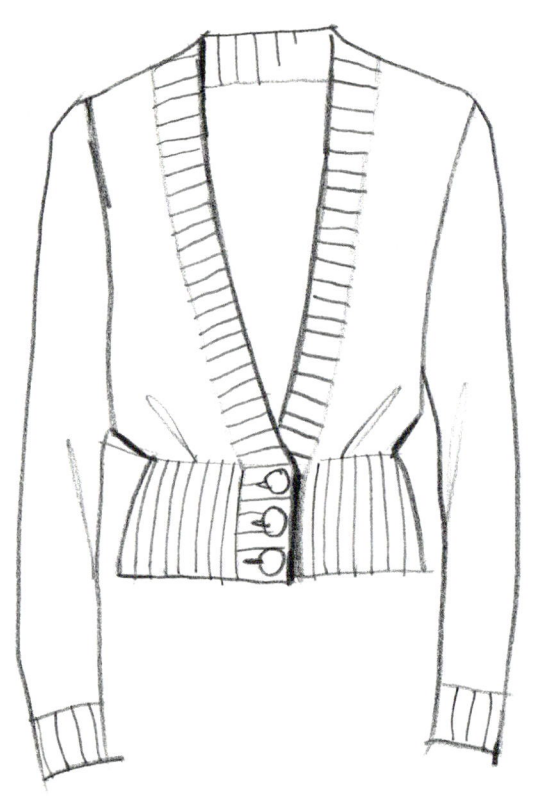

Cardigan buttoned at the bottom

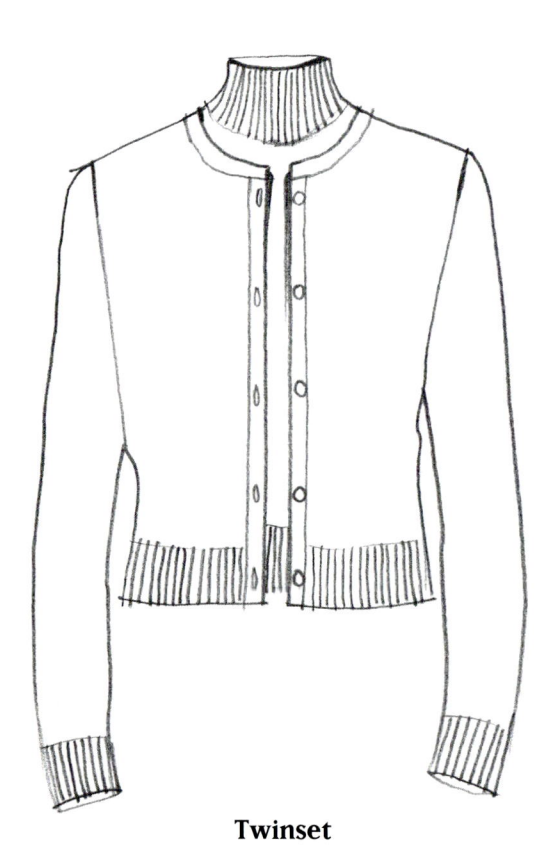

Twinset

Jackets, coats

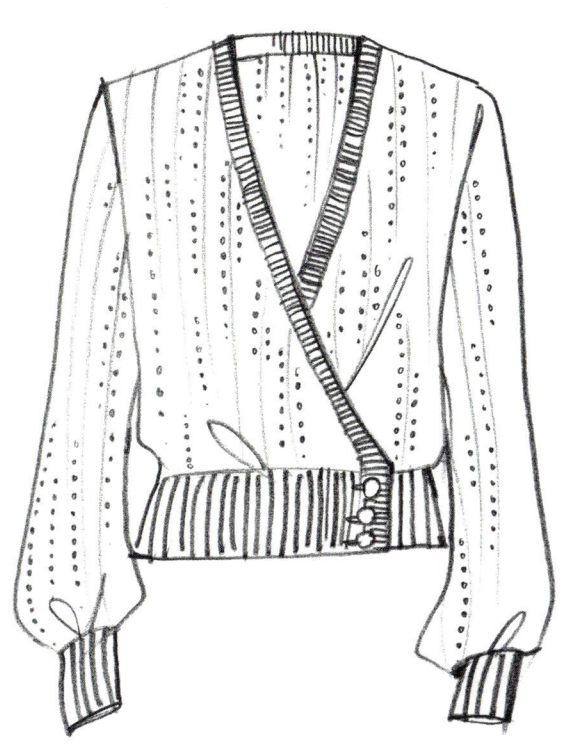

Crossed shed cardigan

Fashioned shirt neckline cardigan

Jackets, coats

Cardigan with applied fabric bow

Handkerchief-style asymetric jacket

Jackets, coats

Montgomery jacket

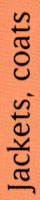

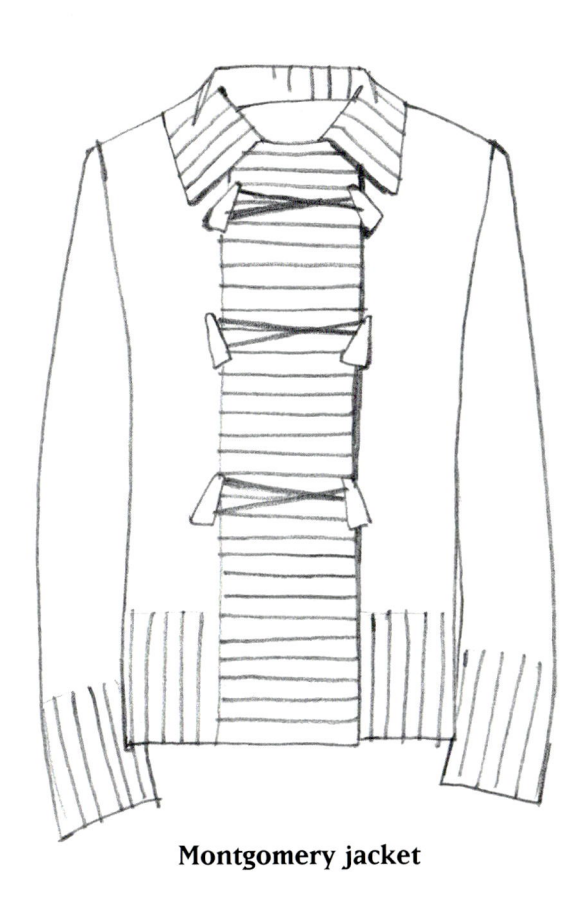

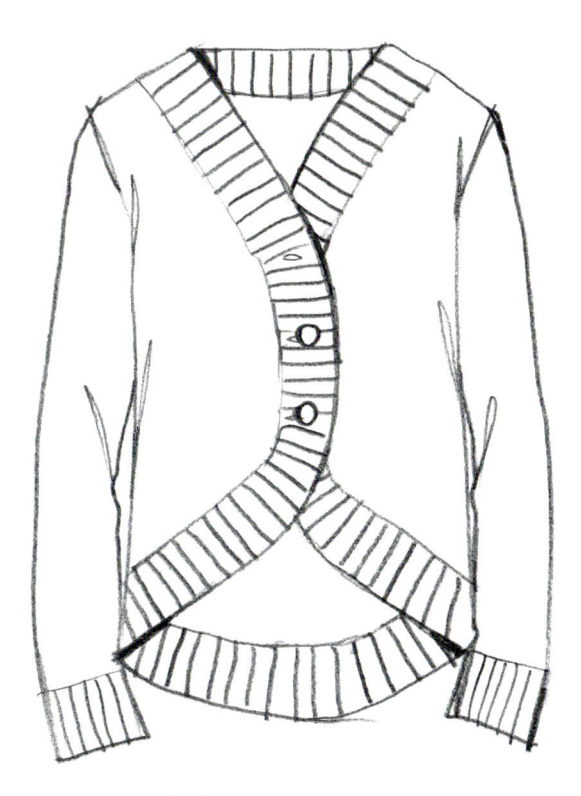

Thick round-cut jacket

Jackets, coats

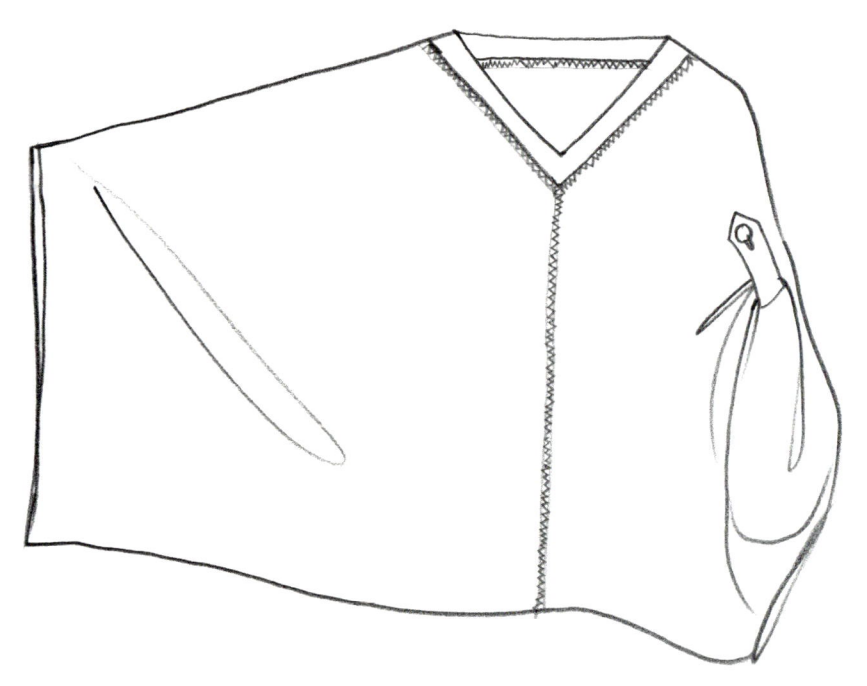

Poncho shirt with covered seams

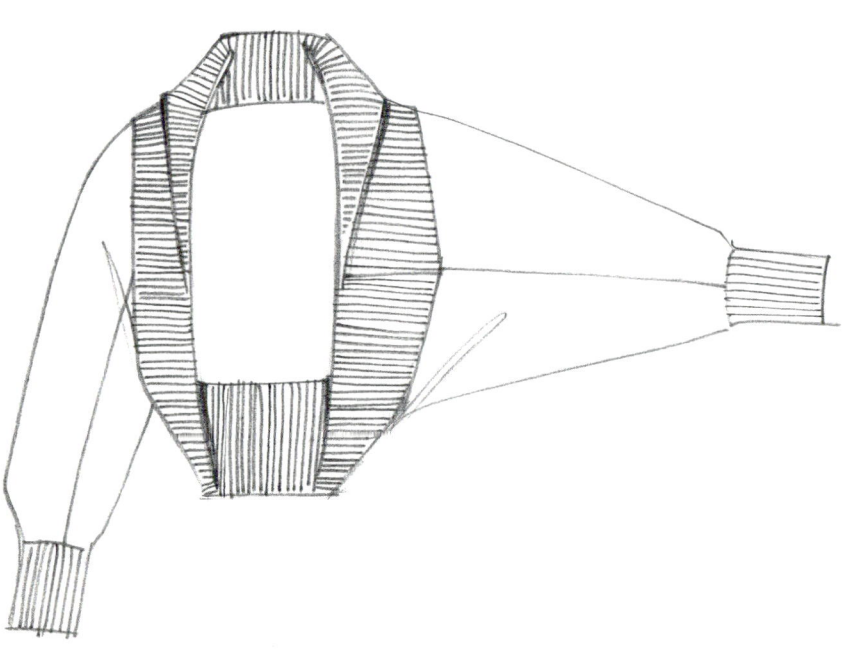

Revised bolero

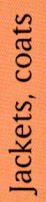

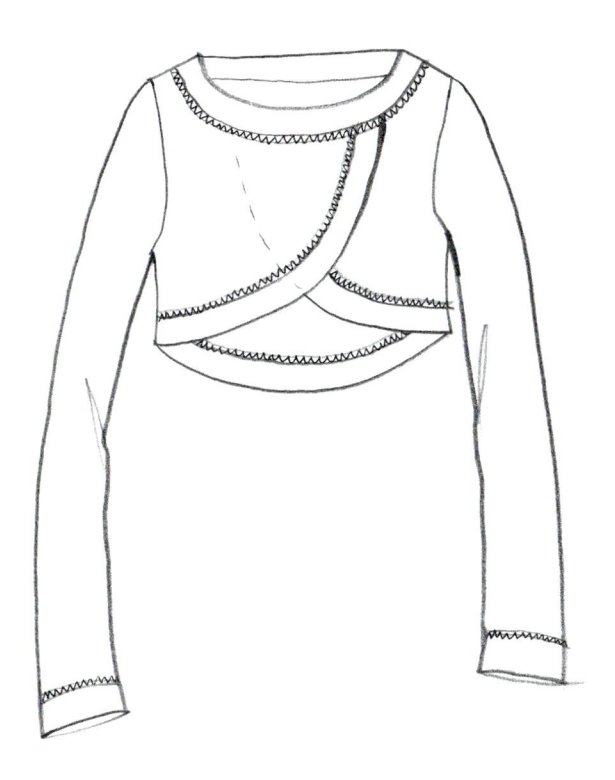

**Micro shirt with overlapped layers
and covered seams**

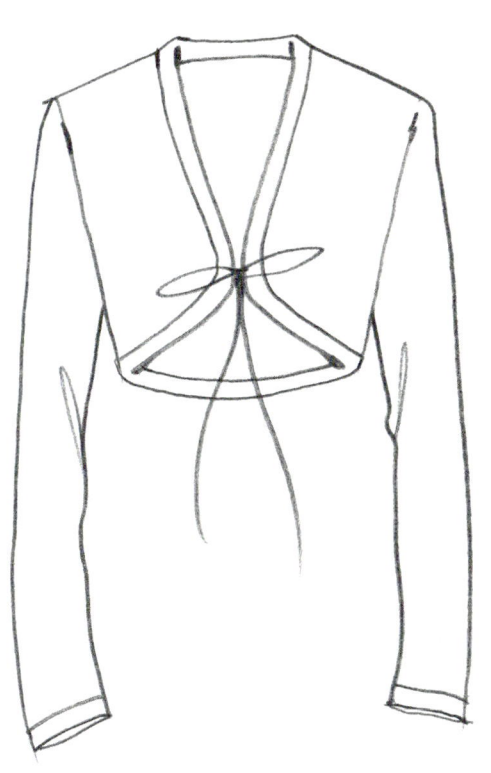

Bolero with bow tie

Jackets, coats

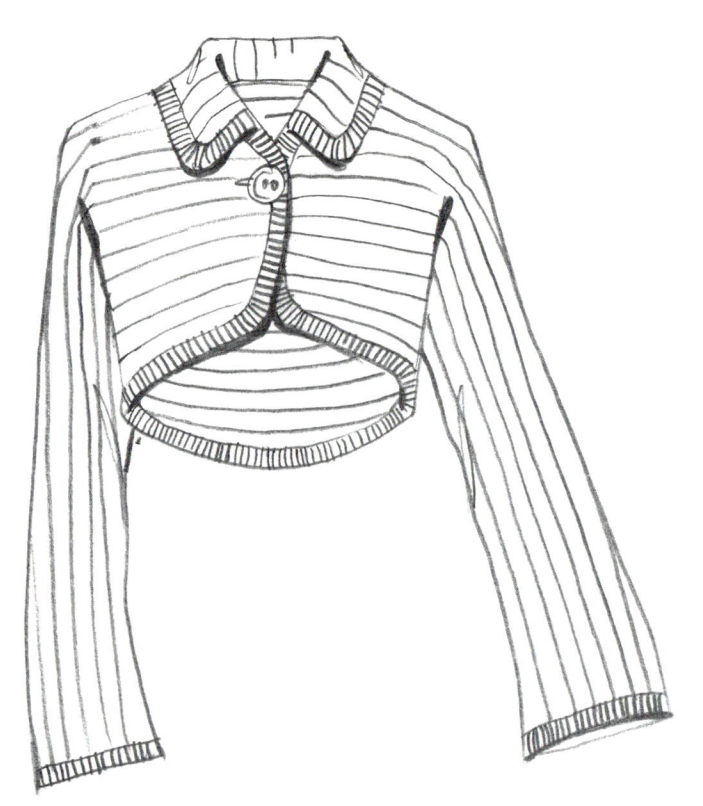

Ribbed bolero with Japanese sleeves

Short and double-breasted cape

Jackets, coats

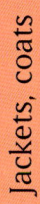

Turtleneck poncho

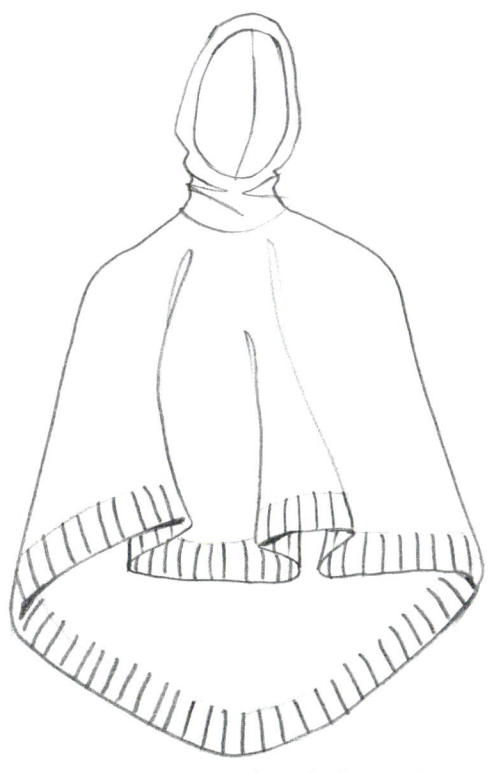

Asymetric hooded poncho

Jackets, coats

Poncho with fringes and belt

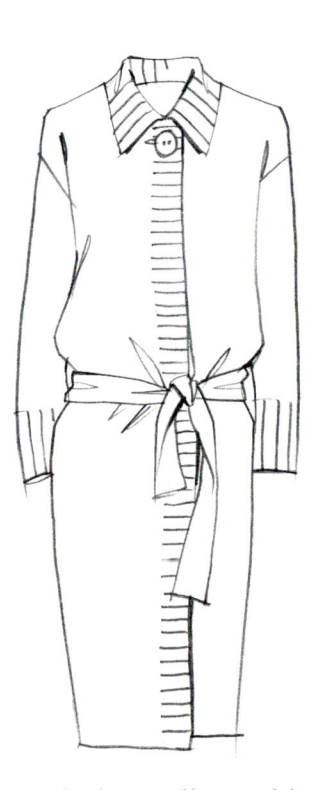

Coat with shirt collar and low cut

Jackets, coats

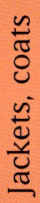

Retro double-breasted compact knitted coat

Thick asymmetric jacket with poof sleeves

Jackets, coats

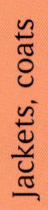

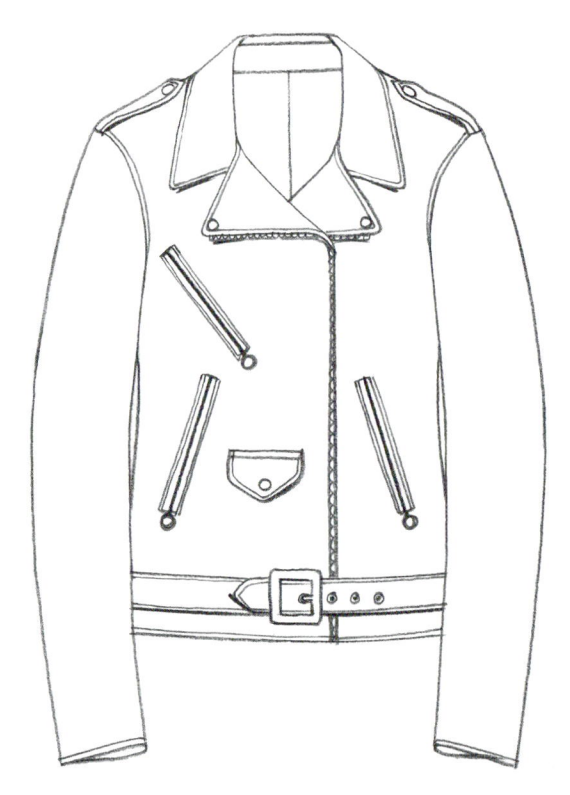

Perfecto jacket (front)

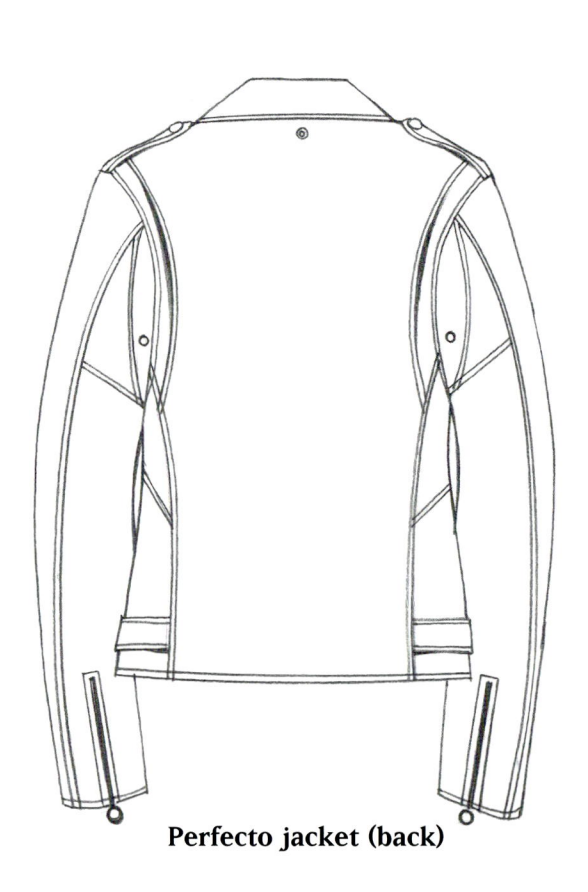

Perfecto jacket (back)

jackets, coats

76

Fitted blazer with tubulars

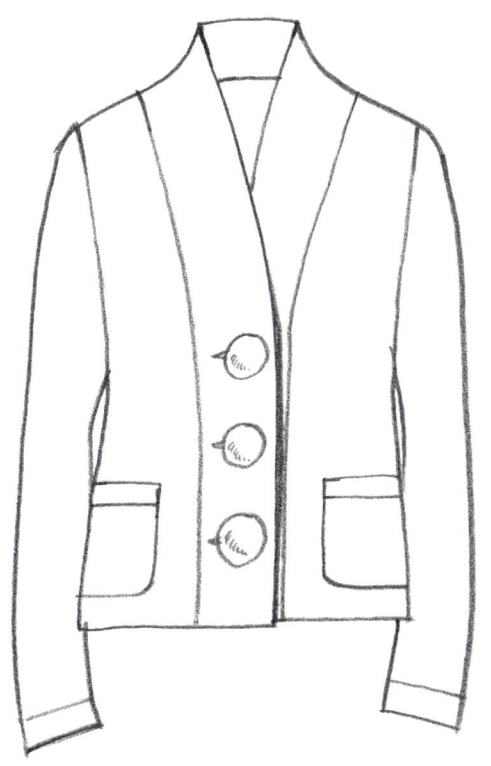

Compact jacket with lined buttons, wide and flat bands

Jackets, coats

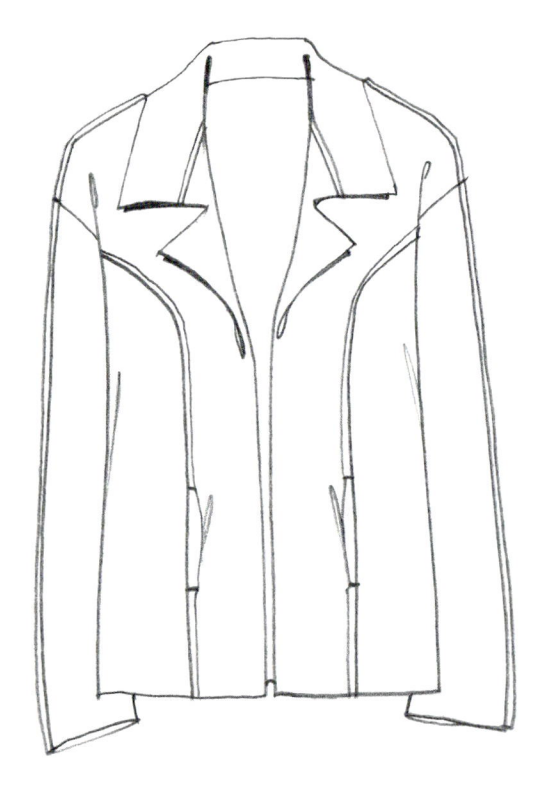

Blazer without buttons and loose seaming

Double-breasted blazer with belt

Jackets, coats

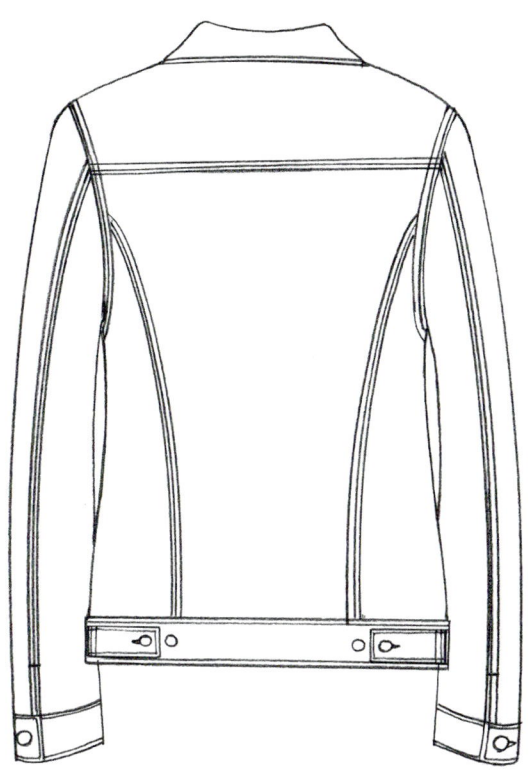

Denim jacket (back)

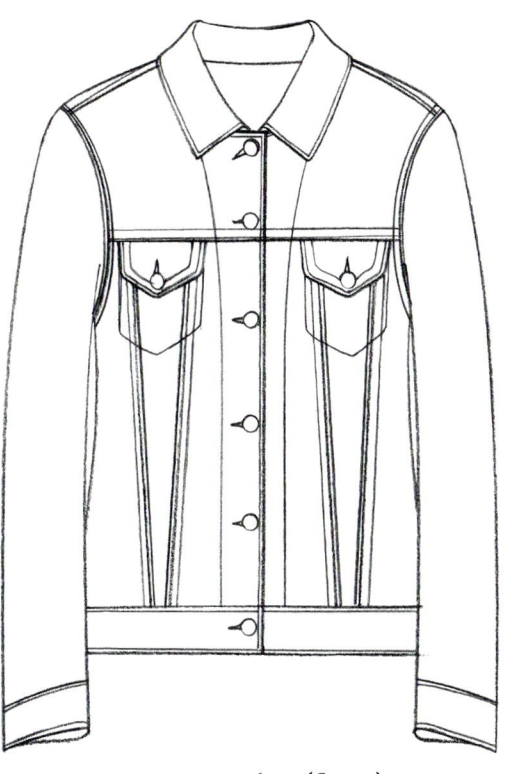

Denim jacket (front)

Jackets, coats

79

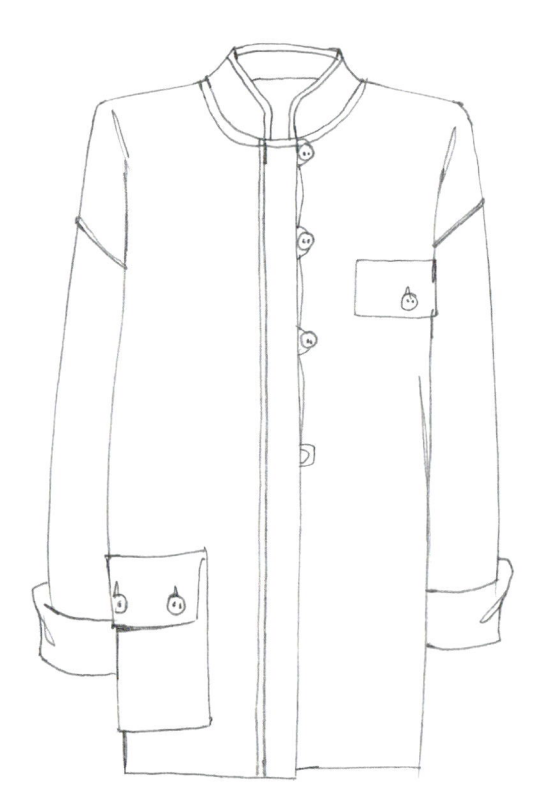

**Large jacket with Mao neckline
and bar tack**

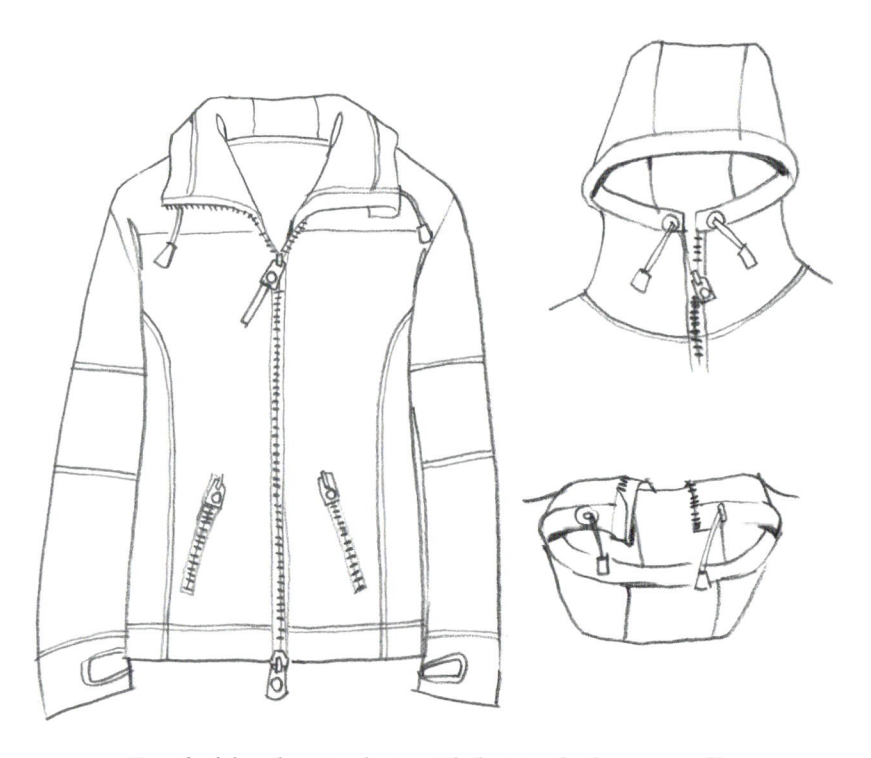

Hooded lumber jacket with buttonholes on cuffs

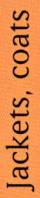

Fleece jacket

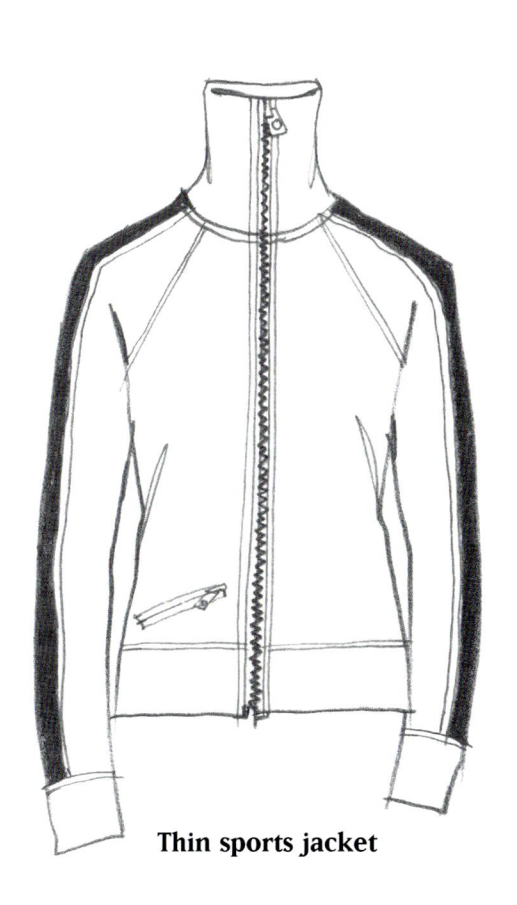

Thin sports jacket

Jackets, coats

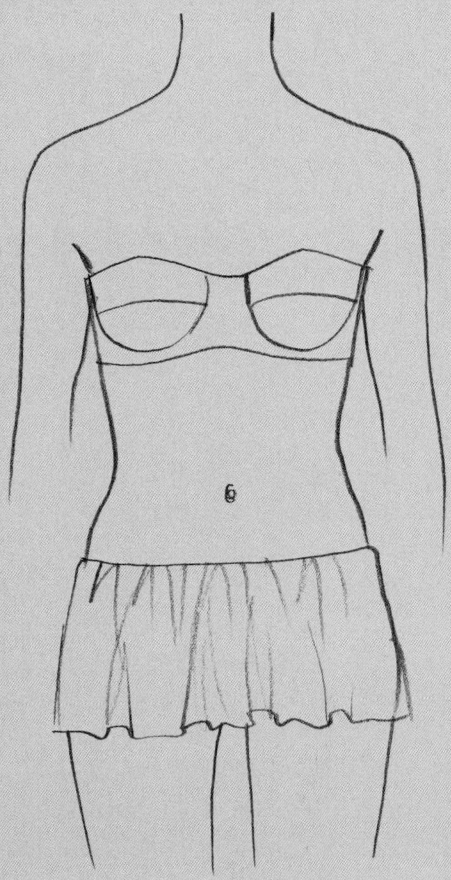
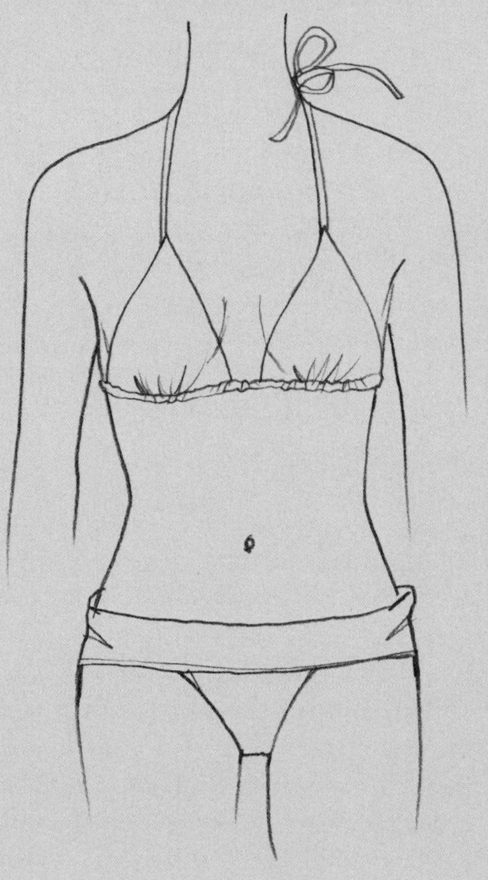
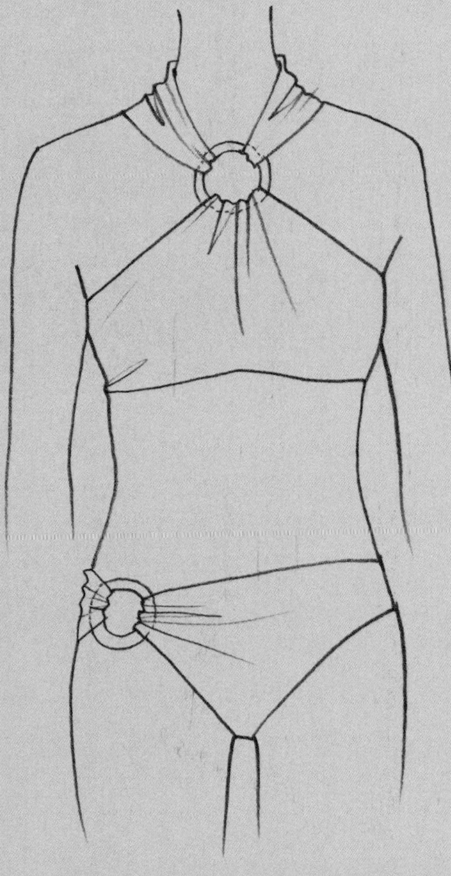
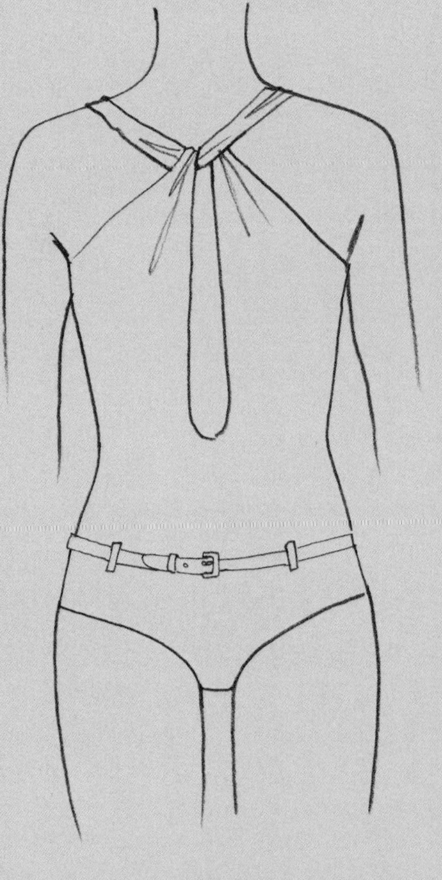

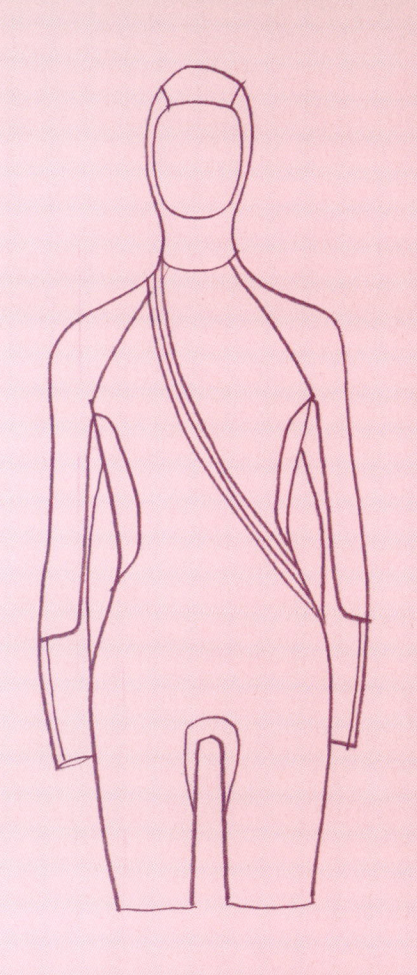

Underwear, swimwear, sportswear

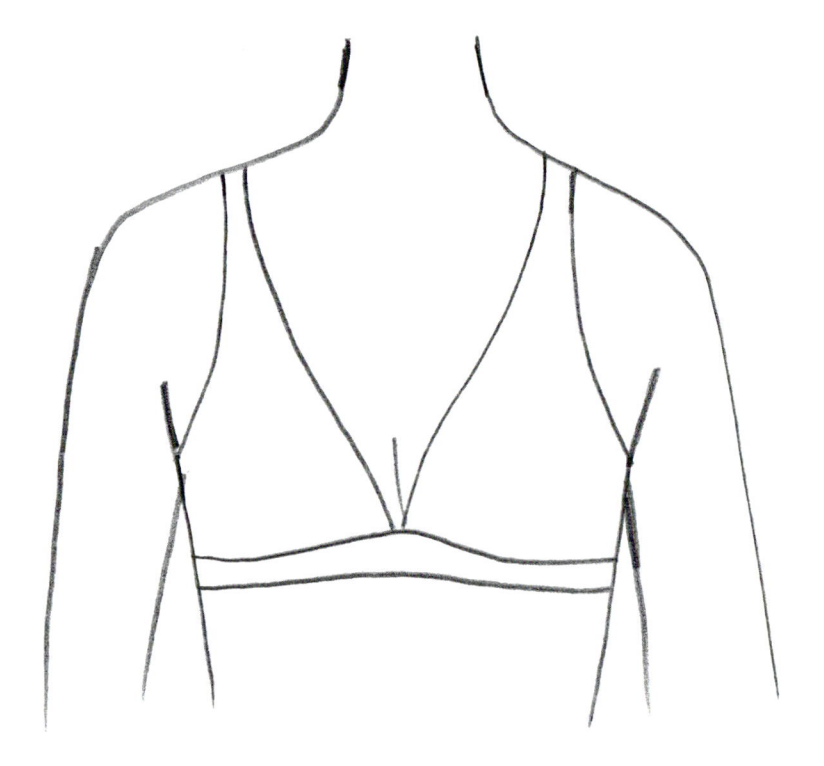

Seamless sports bra

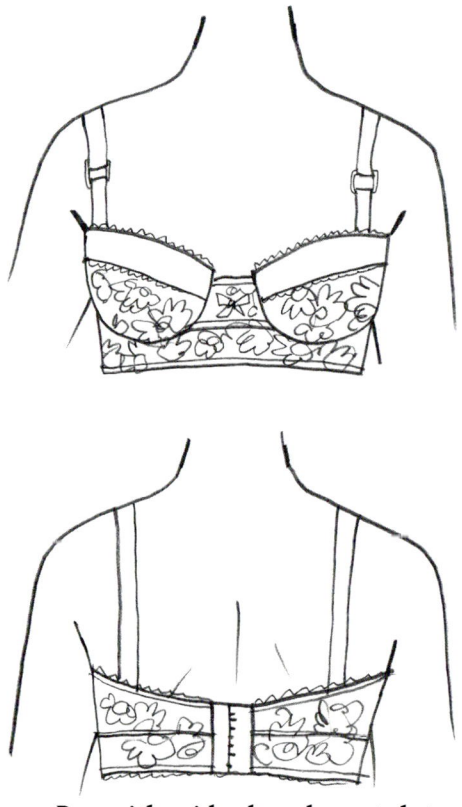

Bra with wide, lace breastplate

Underwear, swimwear, sportswear

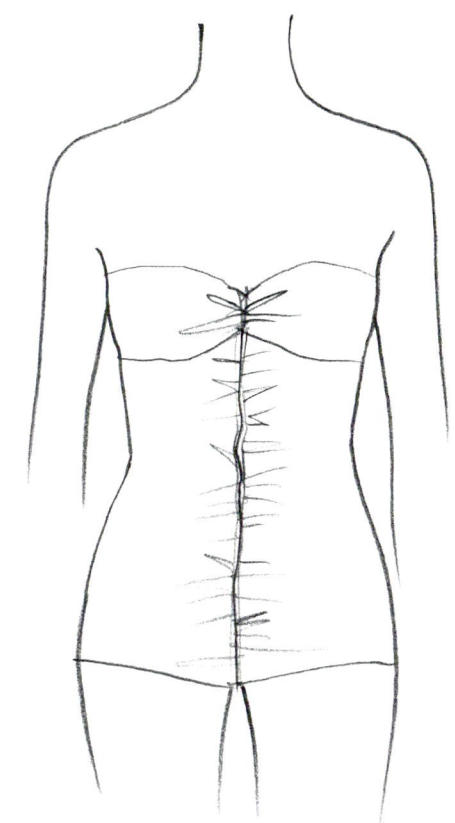

1950s style strapless and gathered bathing suit

1960s style two-piece set with gathered skirt

Underwear, swimwear, sportswear

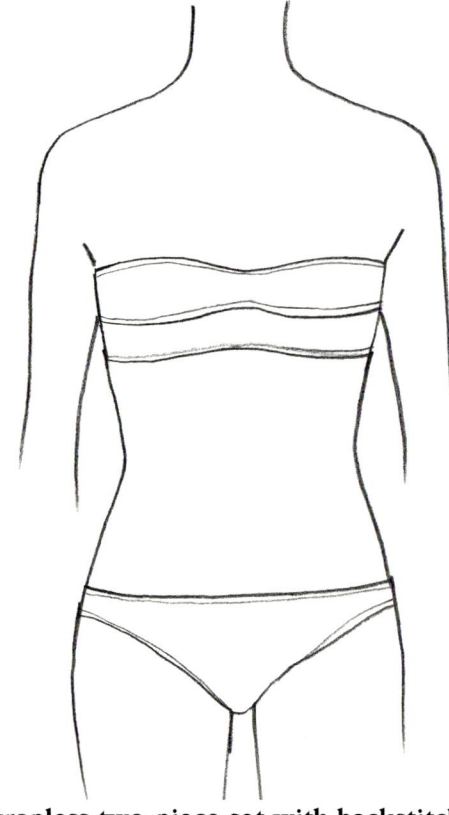

Strapless two-piece set with backstitching

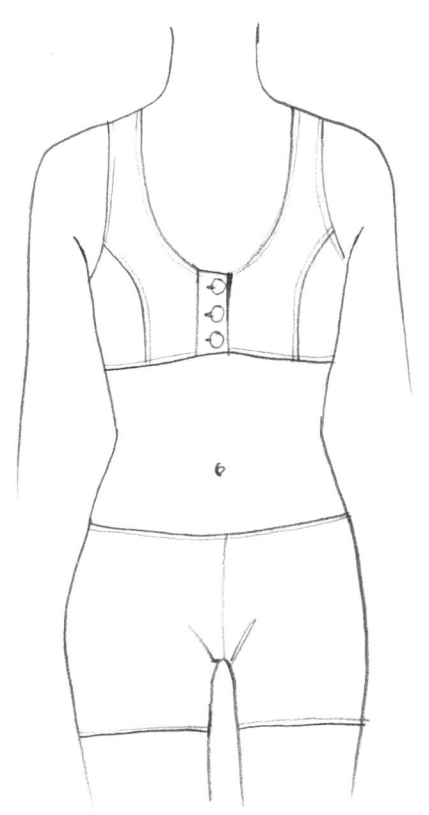

Two-piece set with shorts and backstitching

Underwear, swimwear, sportswear

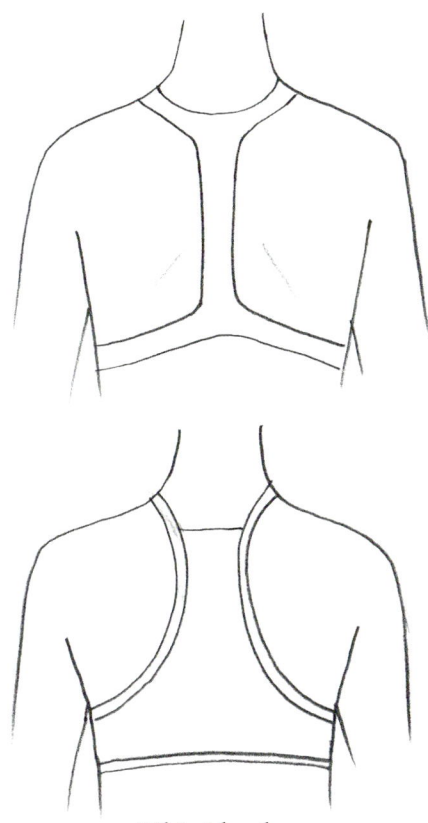

Bikini backs

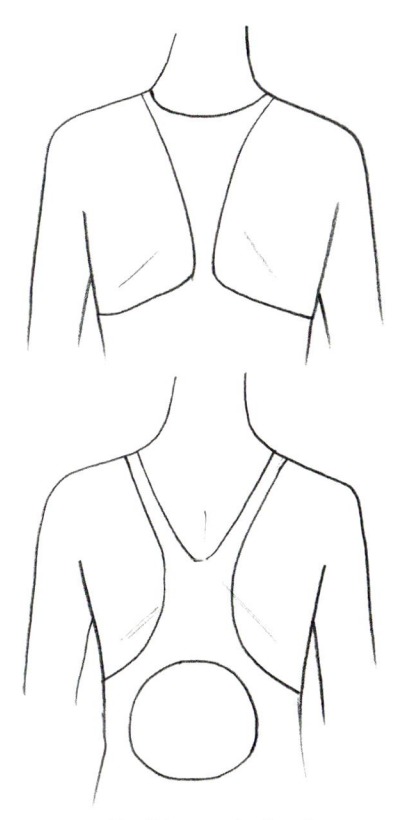

Bathing suit backs

Underwear, swimwear, sportswear

Two-piece set with frills and laces

Two-piece set with turned up panties

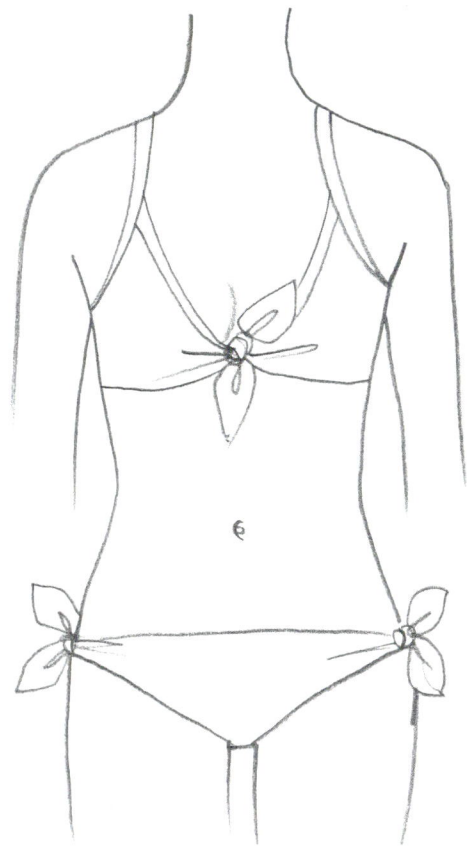

Two-piece set with bows

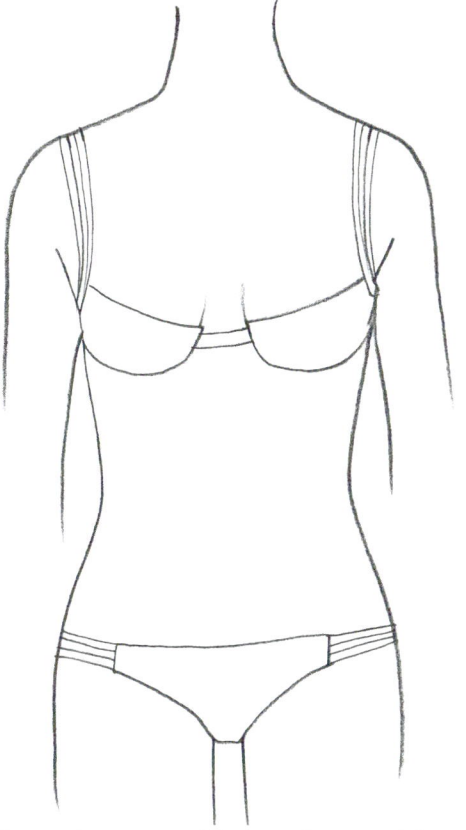

Two-piece set with very low neckline and bands

Underwear, swimwear, sportswear

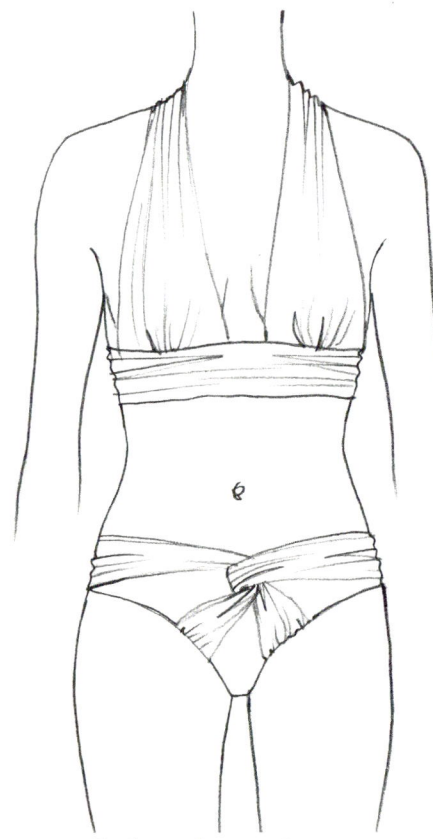

Gathered two-piece set

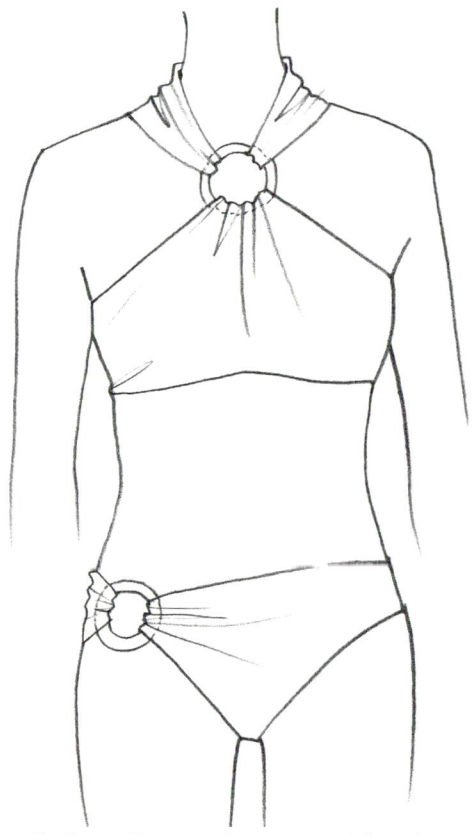

Gathered two-piece set with wire

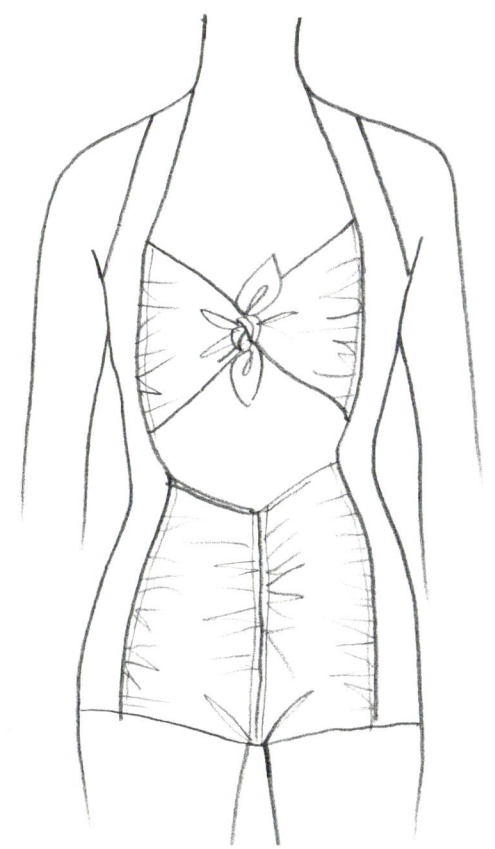

1940s style bathing suit

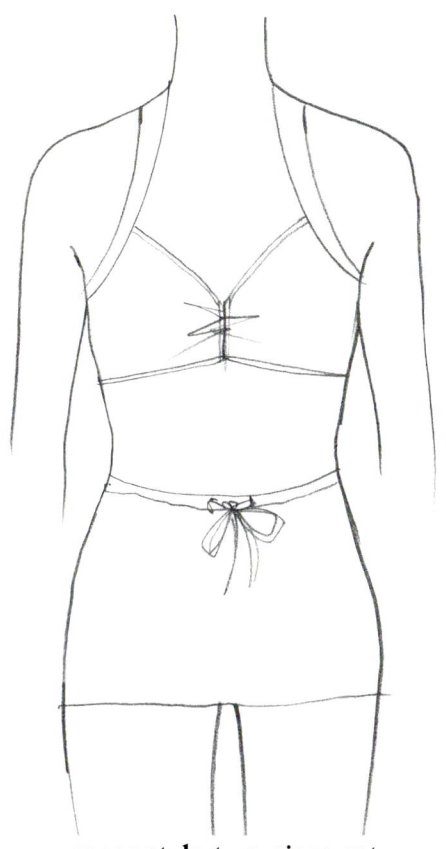

1940s style two-piece set

Underwear, swimwear, sportswear

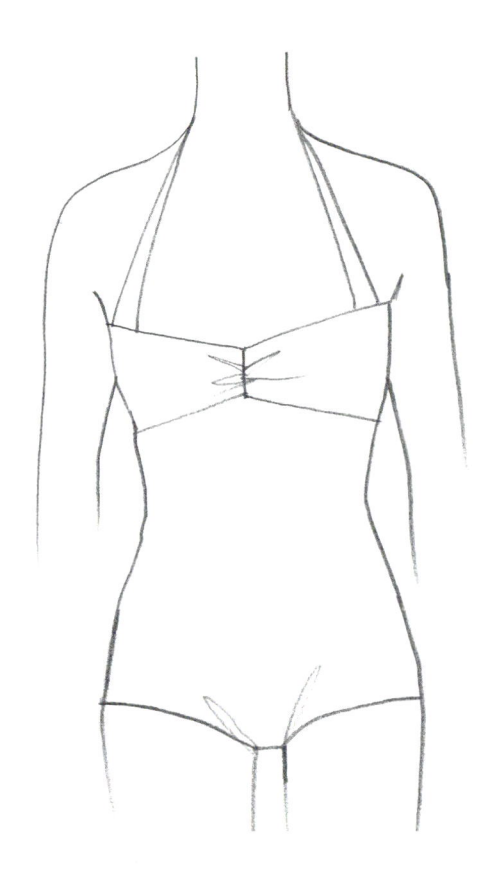

1950s style bathing suit tied at the neck and gathered neckline

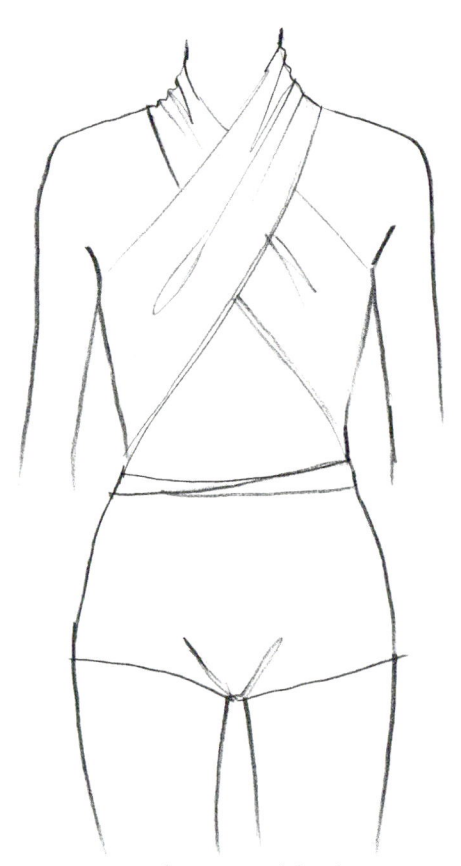

1940s style crossed bathing suit

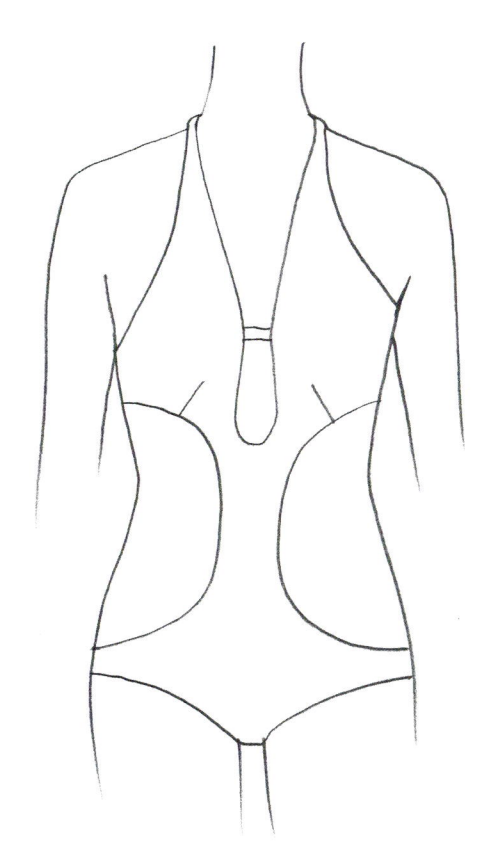

Bathing suit with deep neckline, straps and visible waistline

1980s style bathing suit with lateral bows

Underwear, swimwear, sportswear

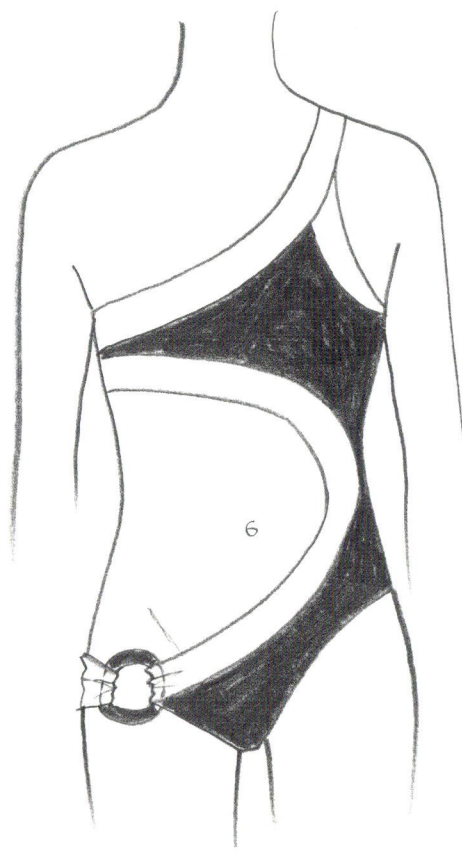

Asymmetric bathing suit with hoop

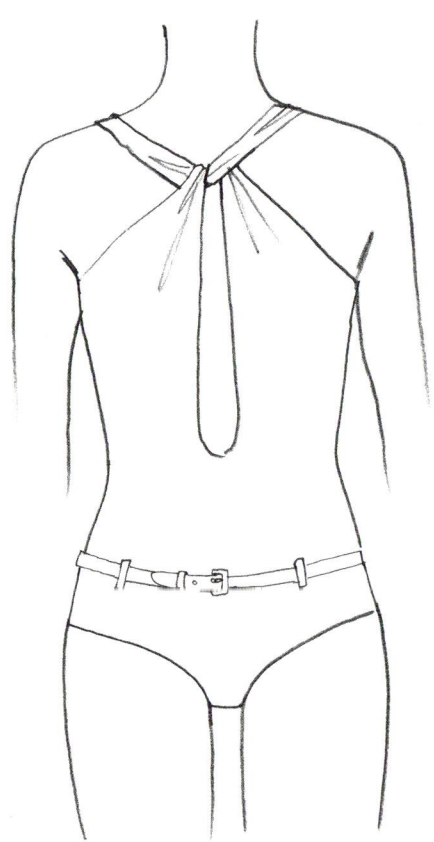

Draped and crossed neckline bathing suit with narrow belt

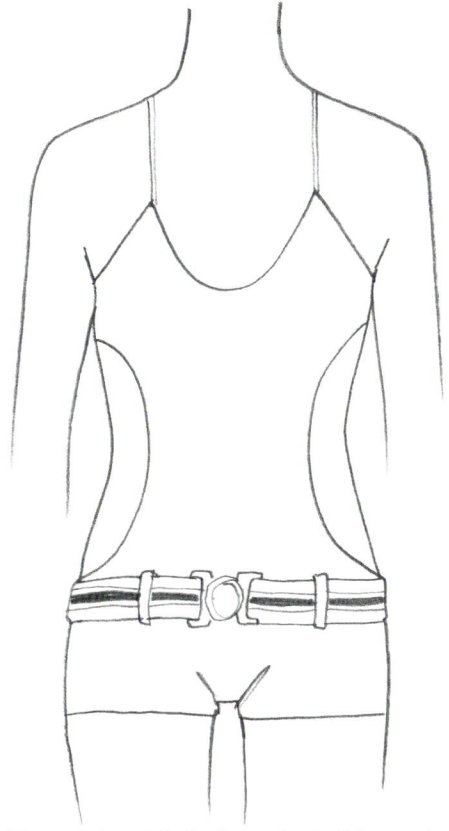

Bathing suit with belt and visible waistline

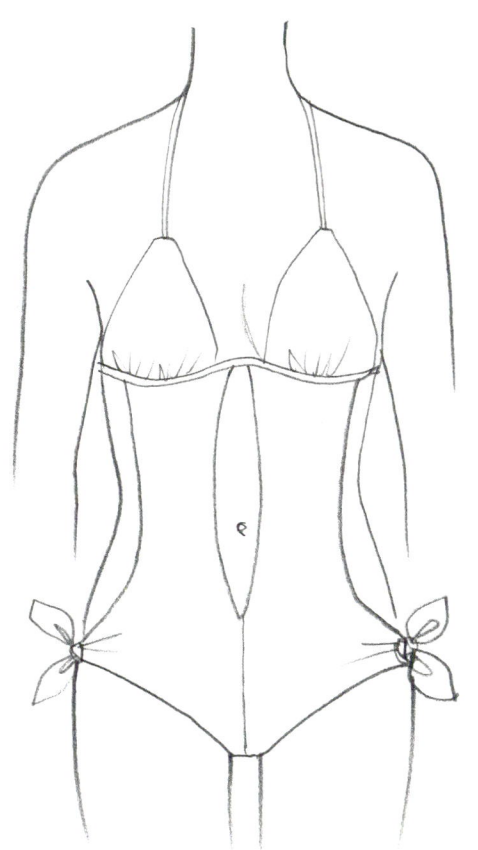

Bathing suit with bows and revealed body parts

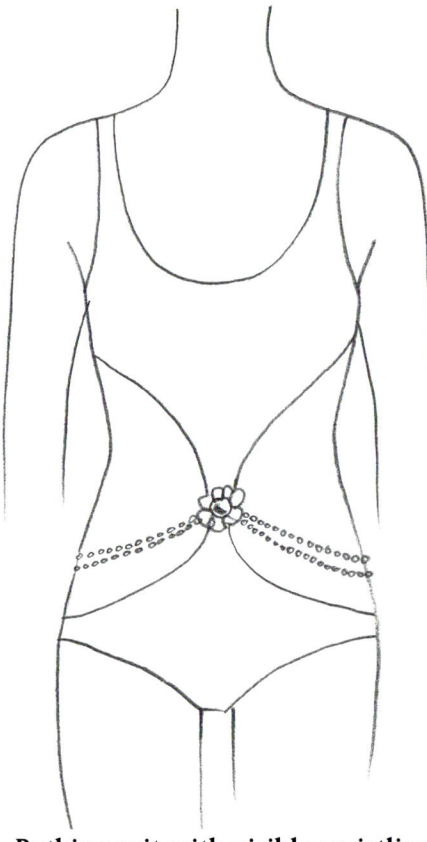

Bathing suit with visible waistline and jewelry

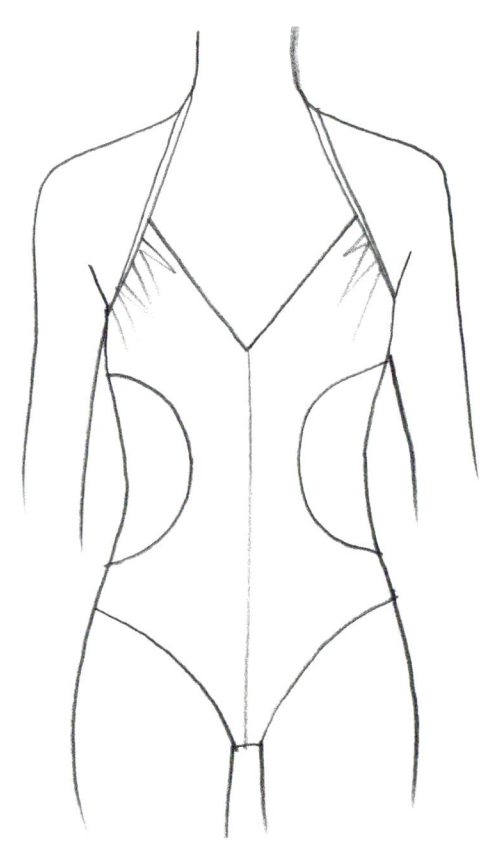

Bathing suit gathered at neckline and visible waistline

Underwear, swimwear, sportswear

96

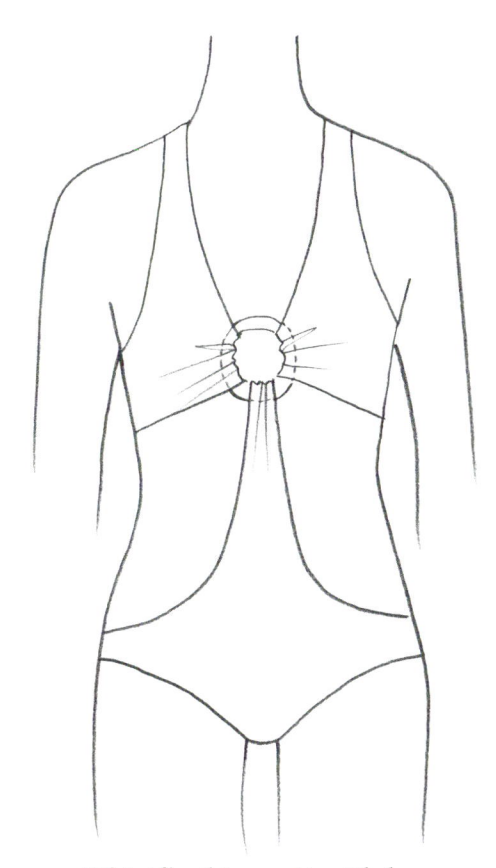

Bikini/bathing suit with hoop and visible waistline

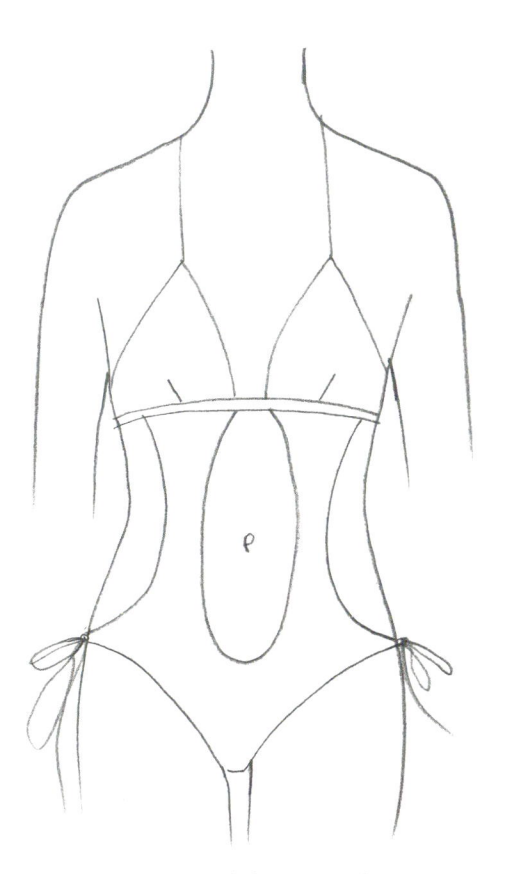

Bathing suit with bows and cut-outs

Underwear, swimwear, sportswear

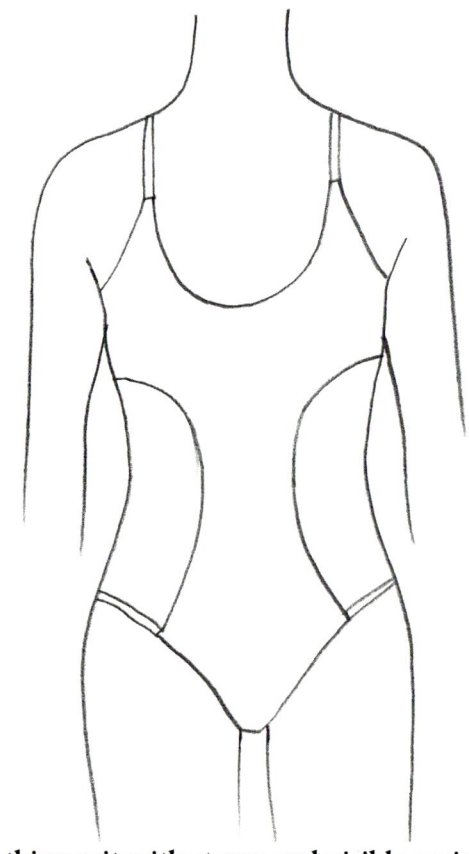

Bathing suit with straps and visible waistline

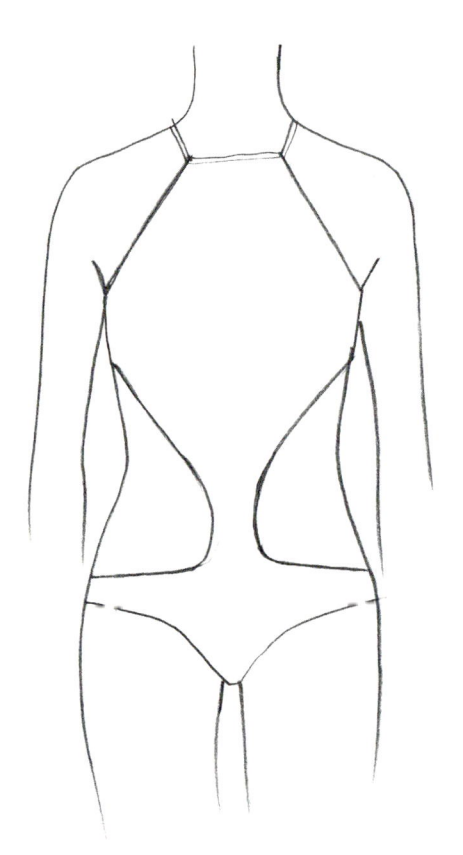

Bathing suit with high and closed neckline, and visible waistline

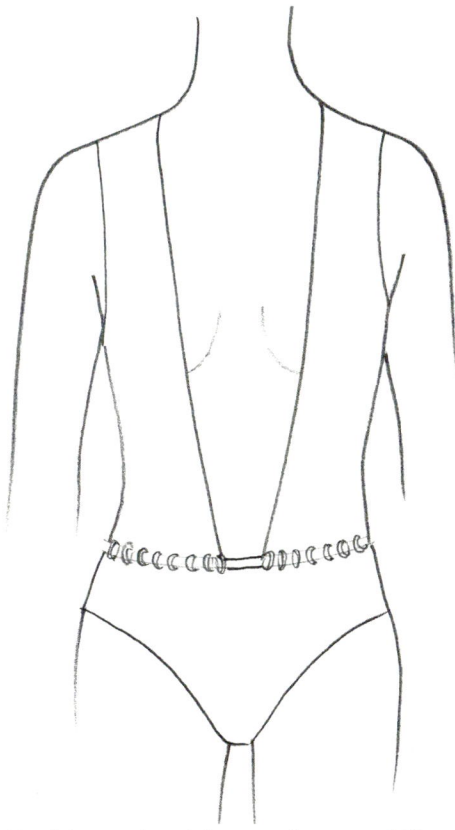

**Bathing suit with very low neckline
and joined by small hoops**

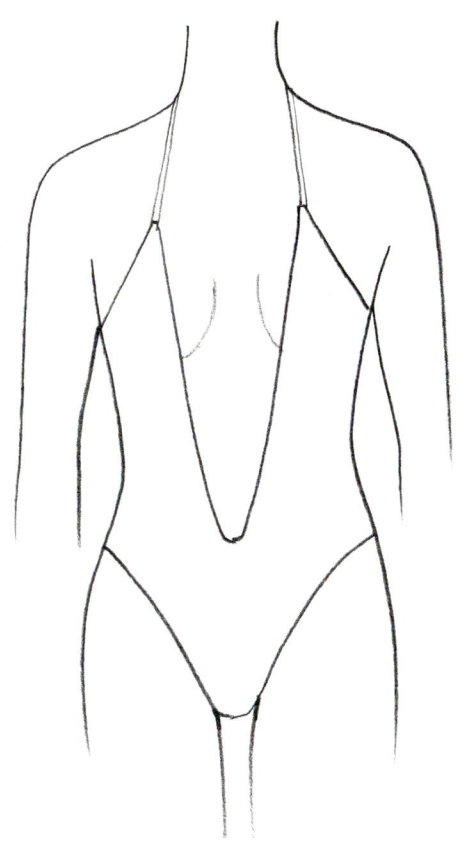

**Bathing suit with low neckline
and taken in at sides**

Underwear, swimwear, sportswear

99

1980s style bathing suit with transparent sections

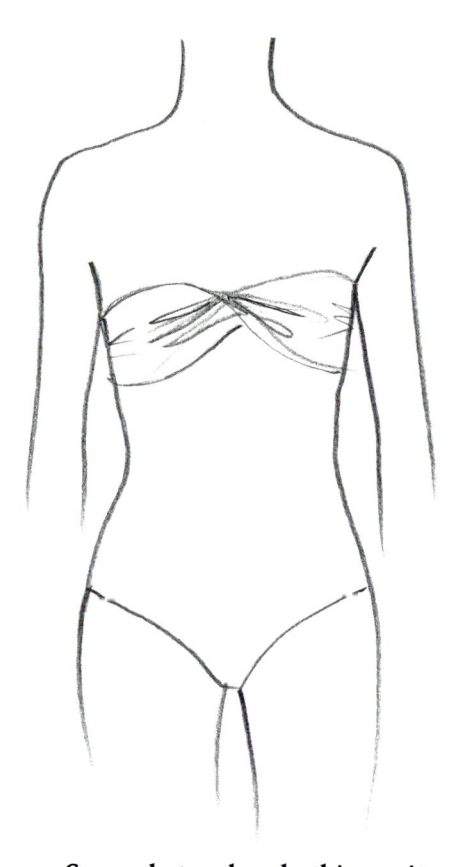

Crossed strapless bathing suit

Underwear, swimwear, sportswear

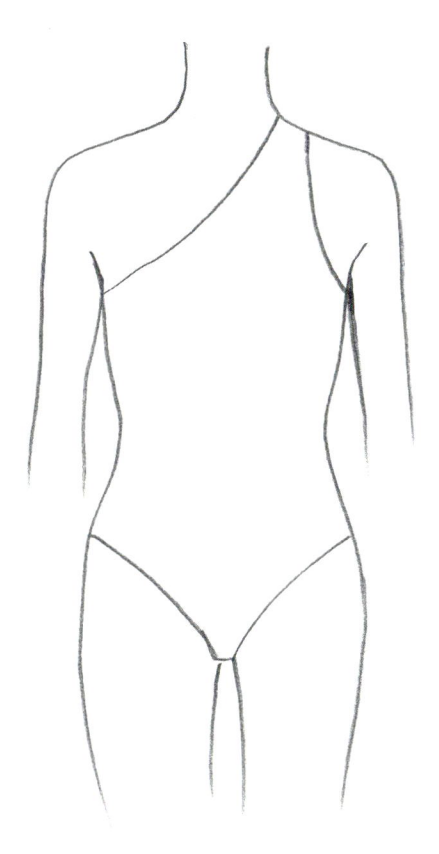

1980s style asymmetric bathing suit

1980s style bathing suit with jewelled straps and crossed neckline

Underwear, swimwear, sportswear

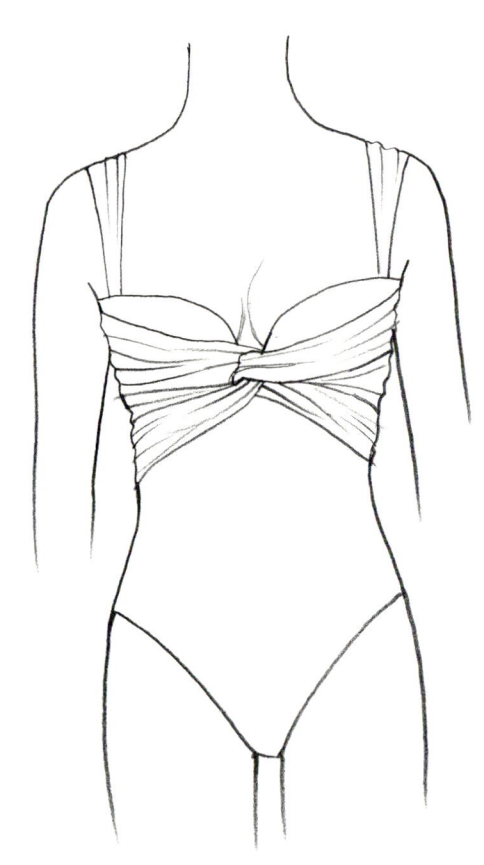

Draped bathing suit

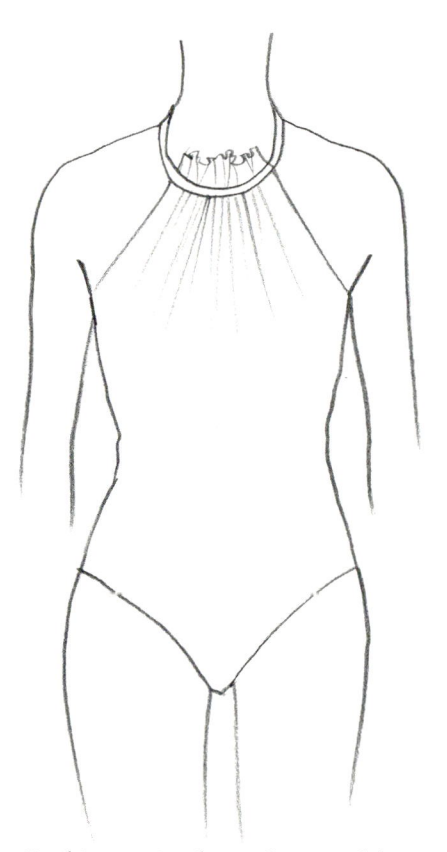

Bathing suit pleated at neckline

Underwear, swimwear, sportswear

1930s style bathing suit in shiny satin fabric

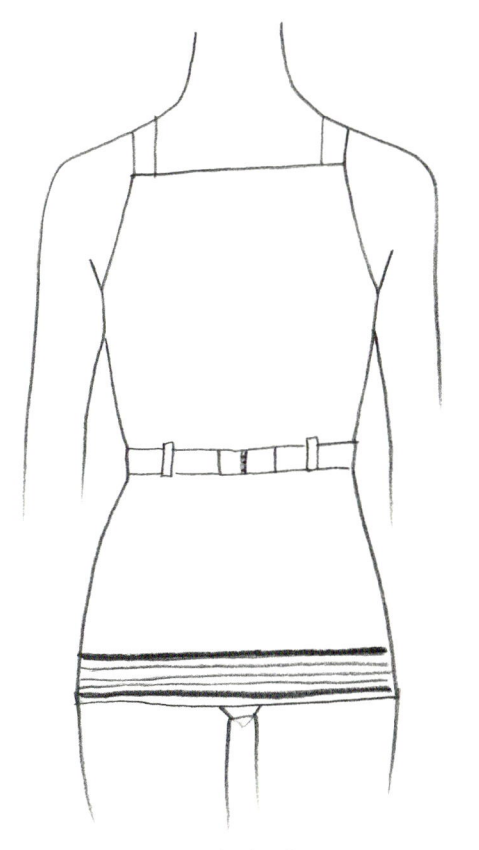

1920s style bathing suit

Underwear, swimwear, sportswear

103

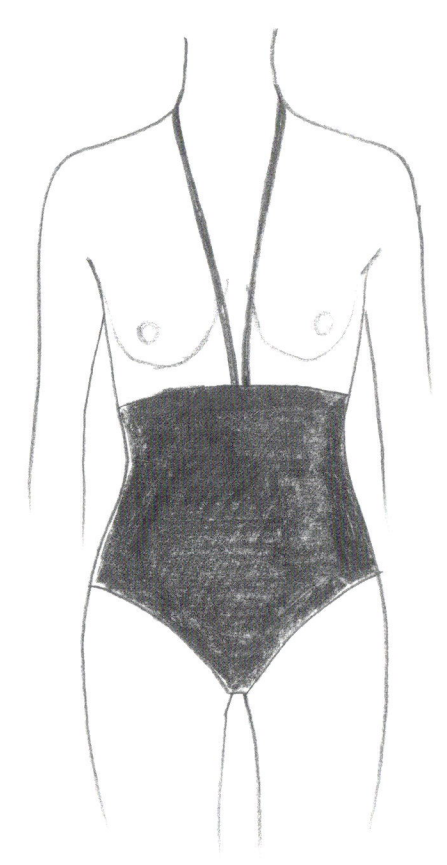

Monokini

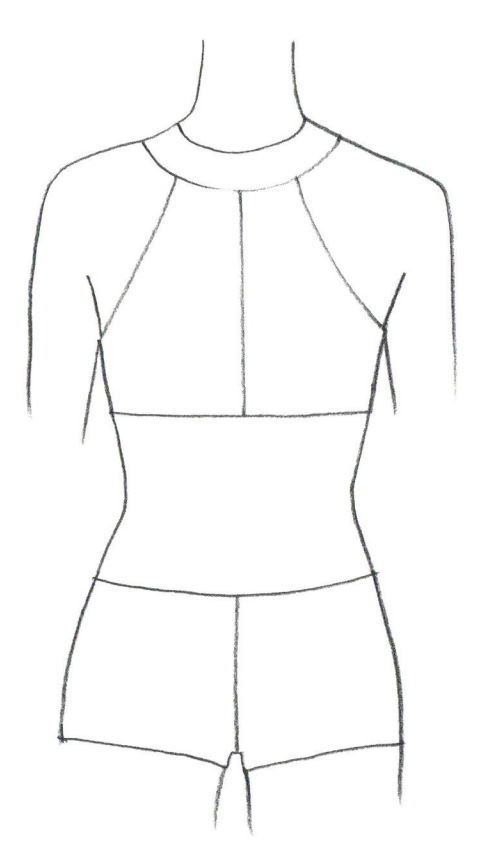

1970s style two-piece set

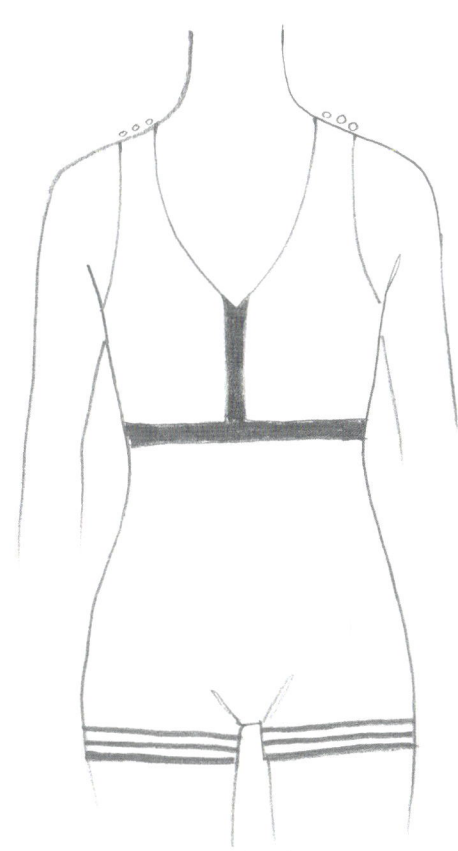

1930s style bathing suit

1930s style bathing suit

Underwear, swimwear, sportswear

105

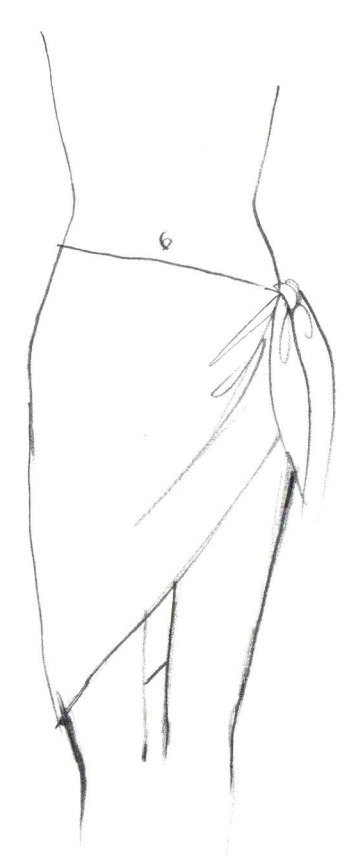

Sarong

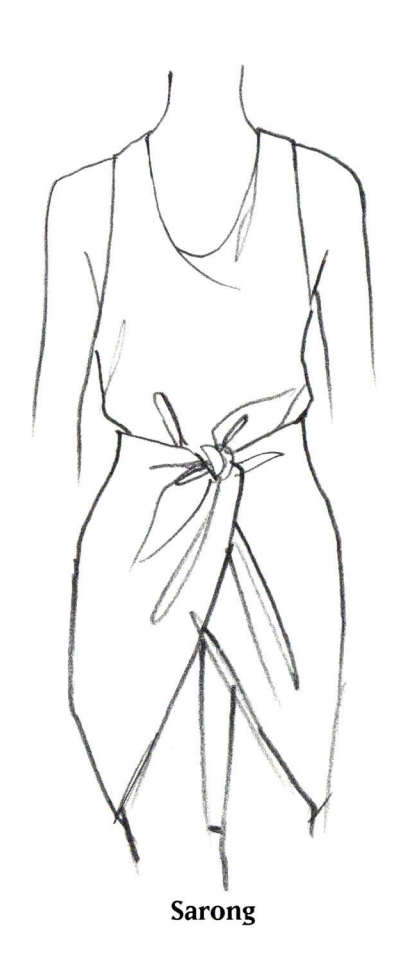

Sarong

Underwear, swimwear, sportswear

Sarong

Sarong

Underwear, swimwear, sportswear

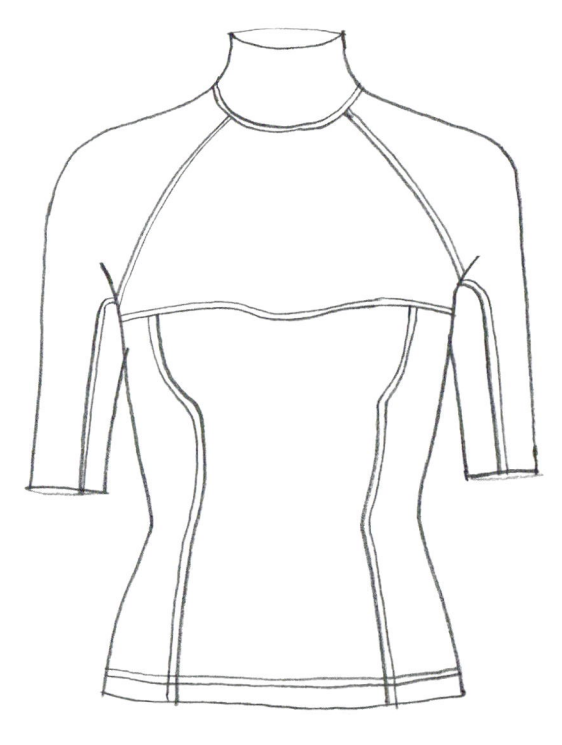

Dive vest

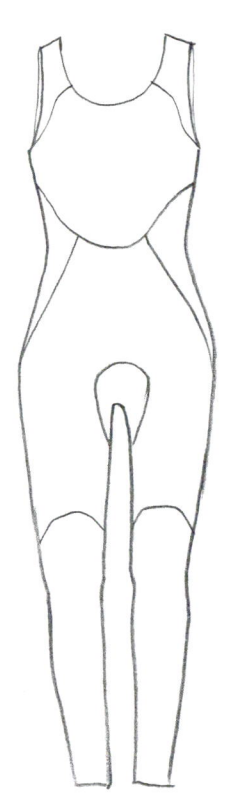

Full-body, sleeveless dive suit

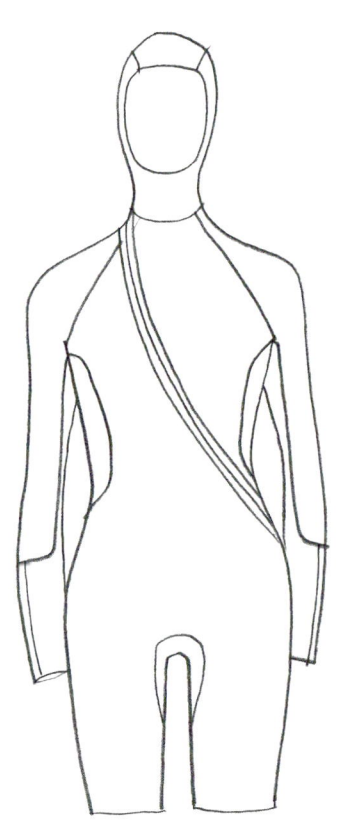

Shortie dive suit

Underwear, swimwear, sportswear

Tennis set

Athletic and boxer shorts

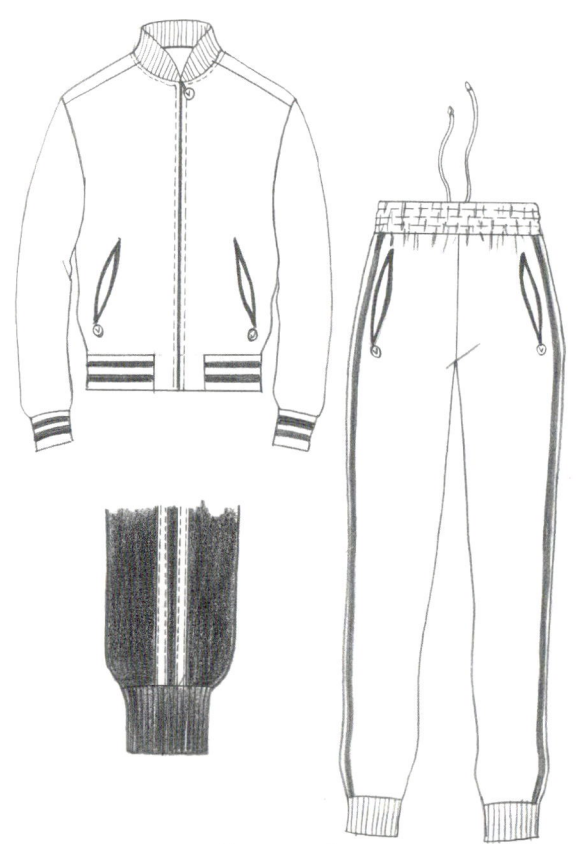

Sweat suit

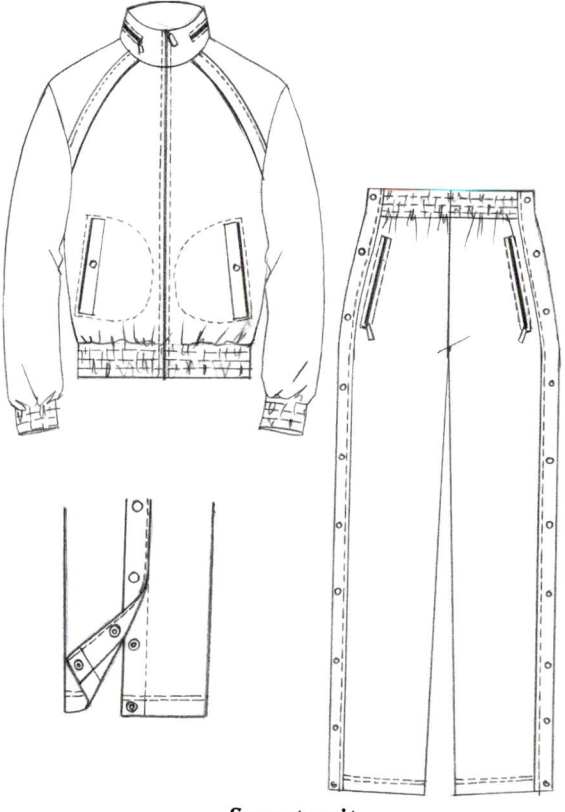

Sweat suit

Underwear, swimwear, sportswear

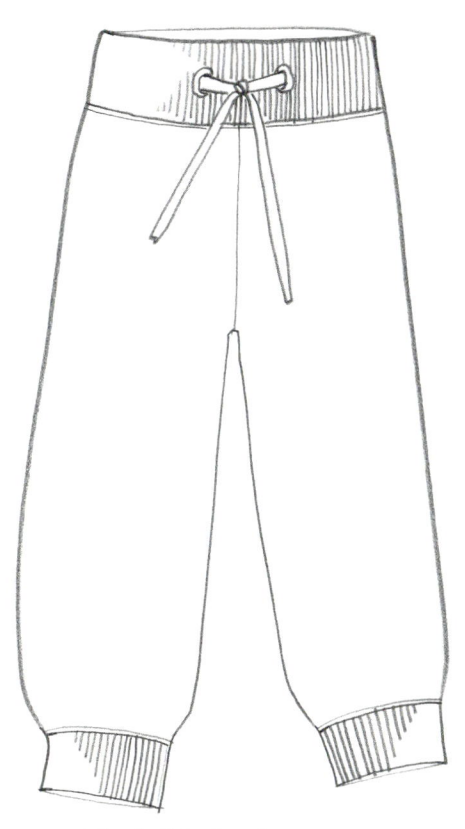

Plush fabric pirate pants

Hooded sweatshirt

Underwear, swimwear, sportswear

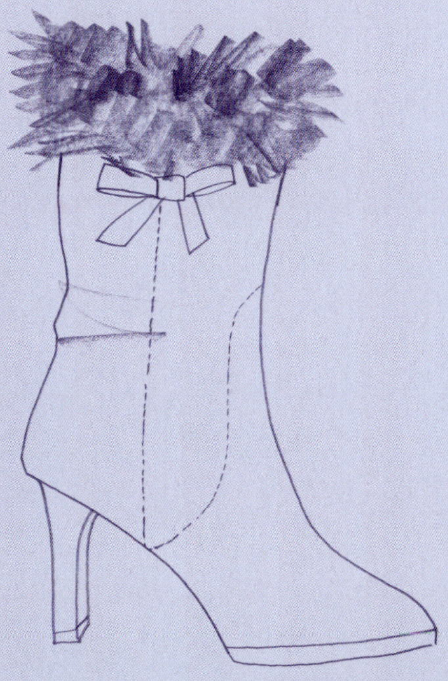
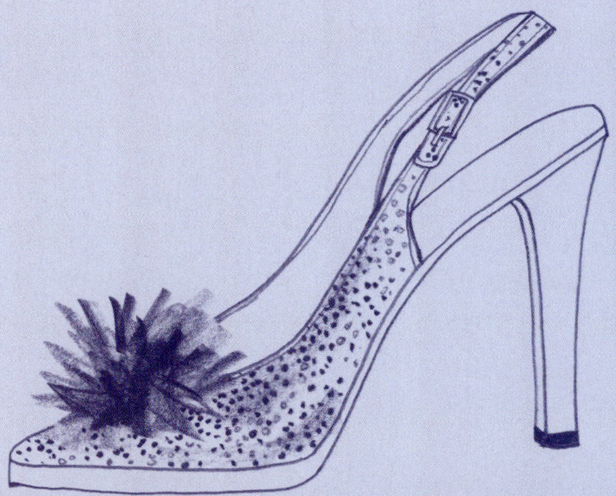
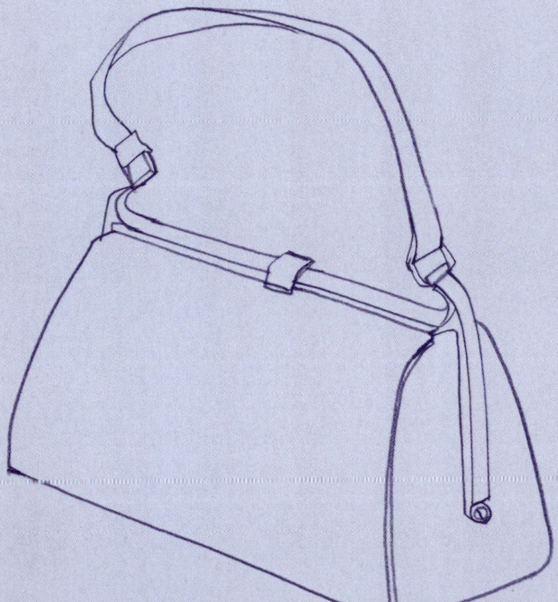
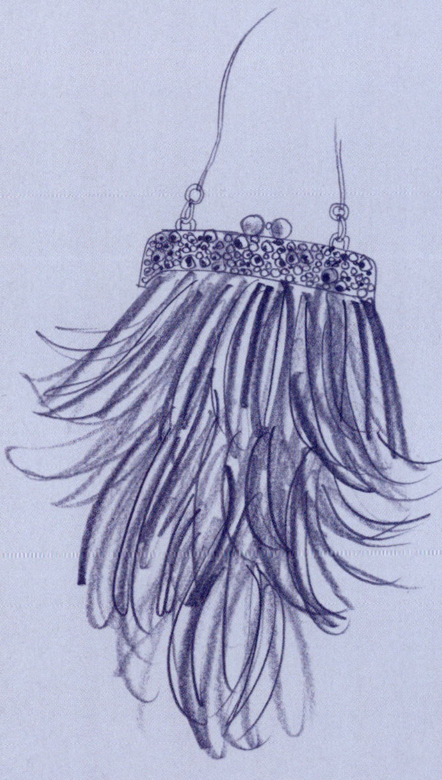

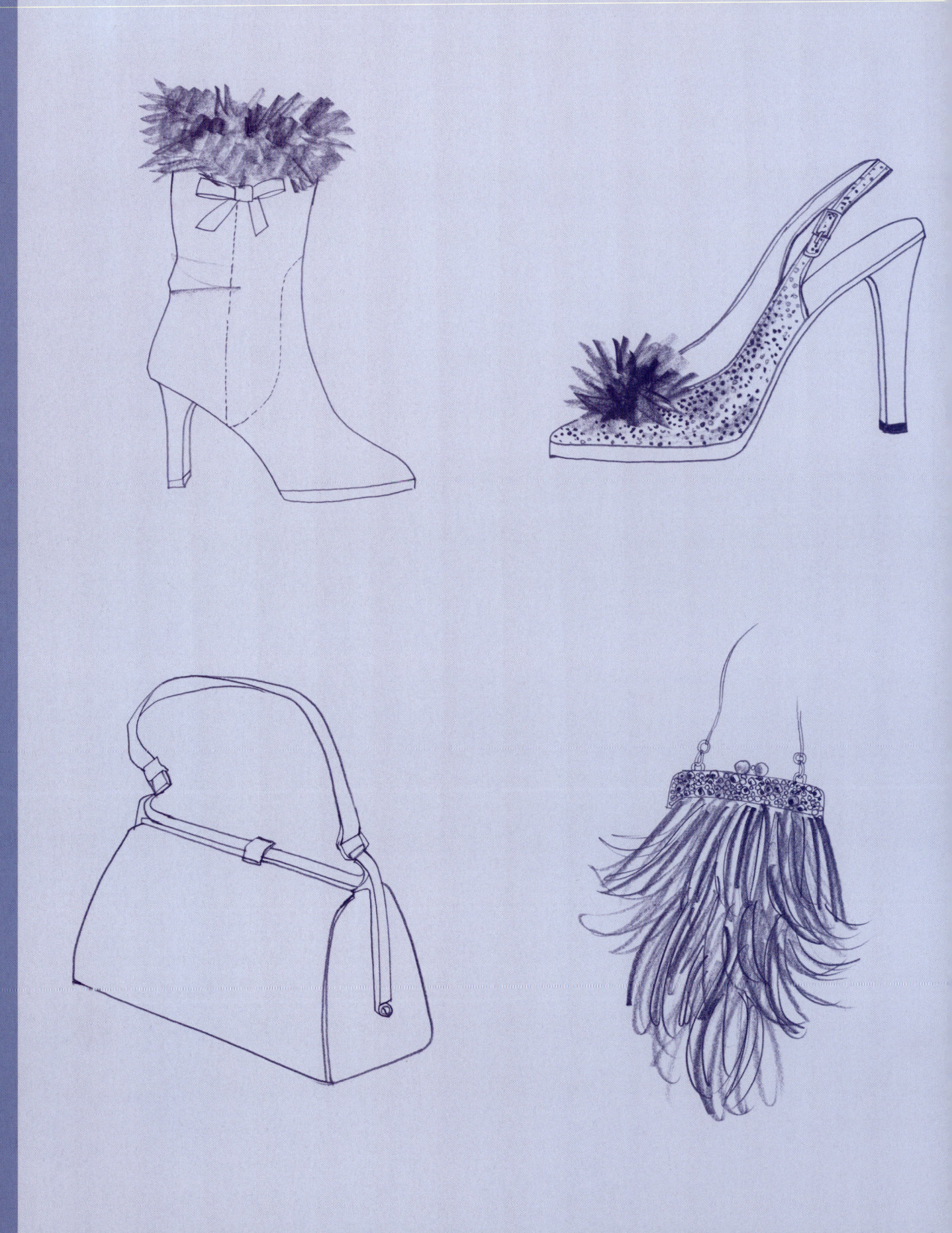

Accessories

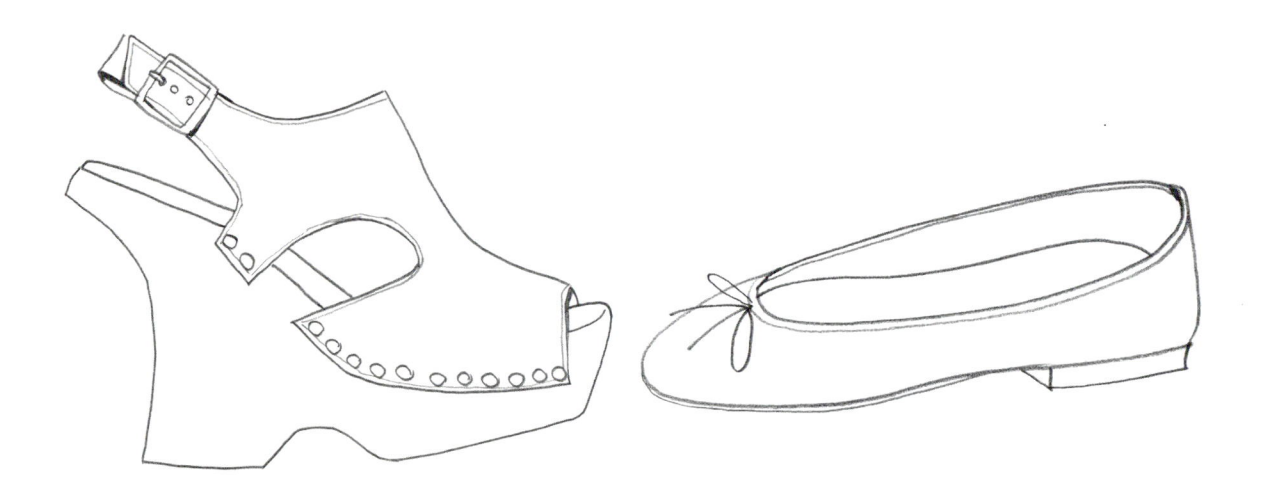

1970s style clog

Ballet flat shoe

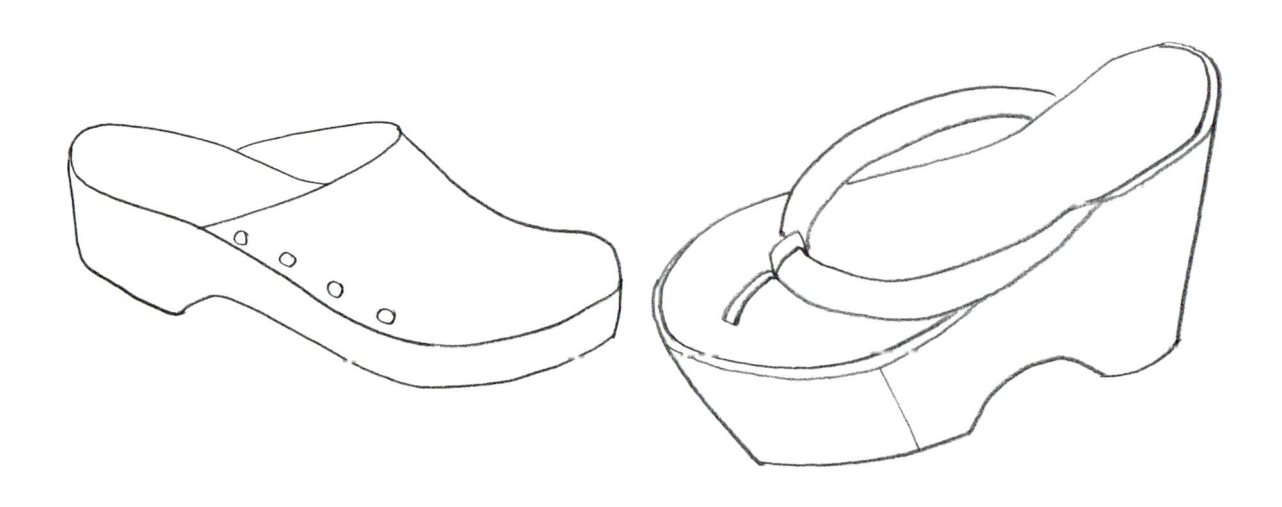

Clog

Revised Japanese clog

Accessories

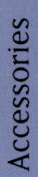

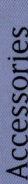

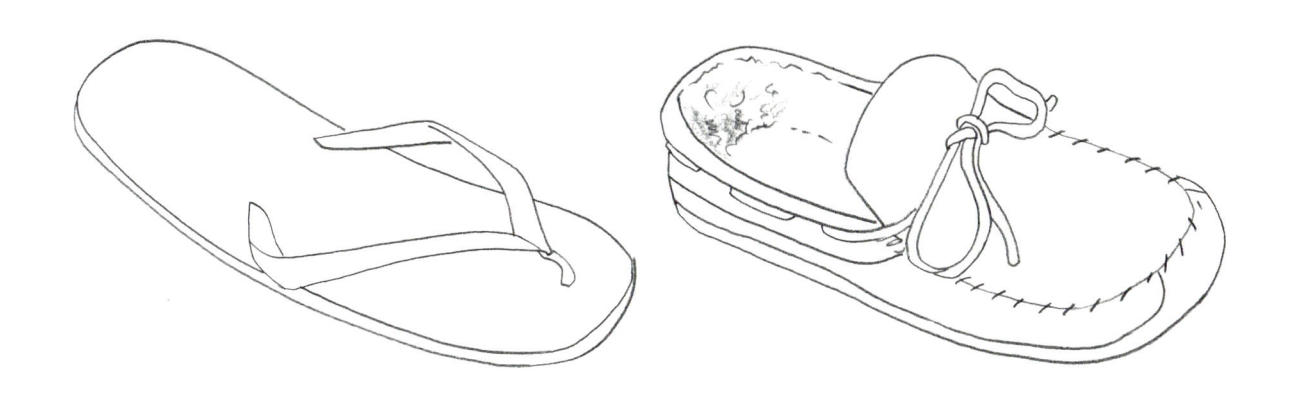

Flip-flop

Moccasin

Exercise sandal

Classic Oxford shoe

Accessories

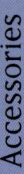

Sports shoe with Velcro

Sports shoe with laces

High-top sneaker

Beach shoe

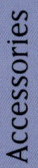

Cowboy boot

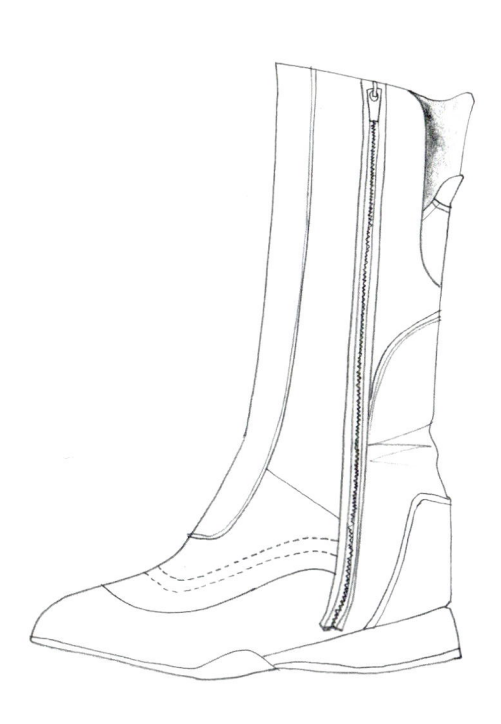

Calf-length boot

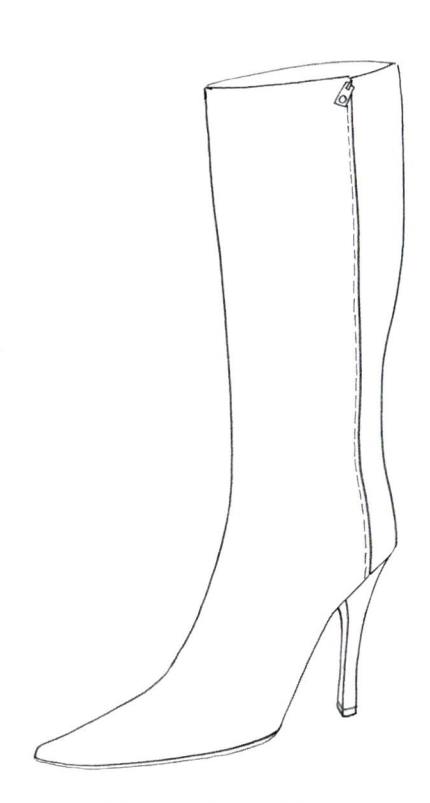

Narrow-legged boot

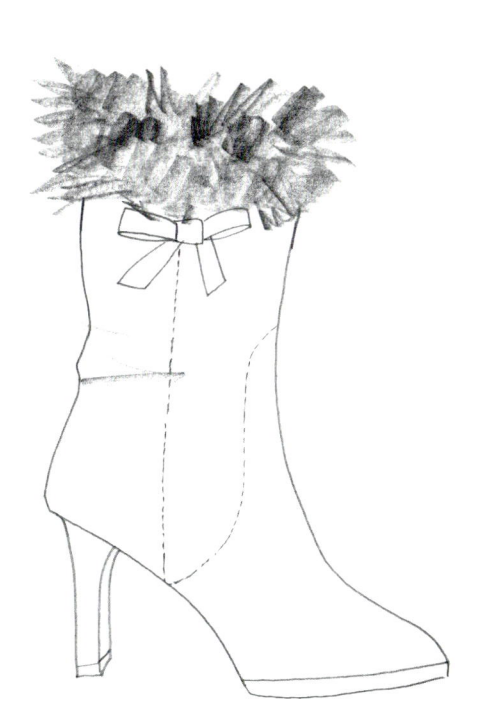

Fur bootee

Accessories

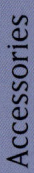

Beaded sandal

Pump with open sides and jewel decoration

Retro perforated pump

Pump with sequins and net flower

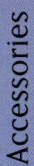

Evening sandal

1970s style sandal

Platform sandal

Retro, gathered pump with strap

Accessories

Bag with scarf

Printed bag

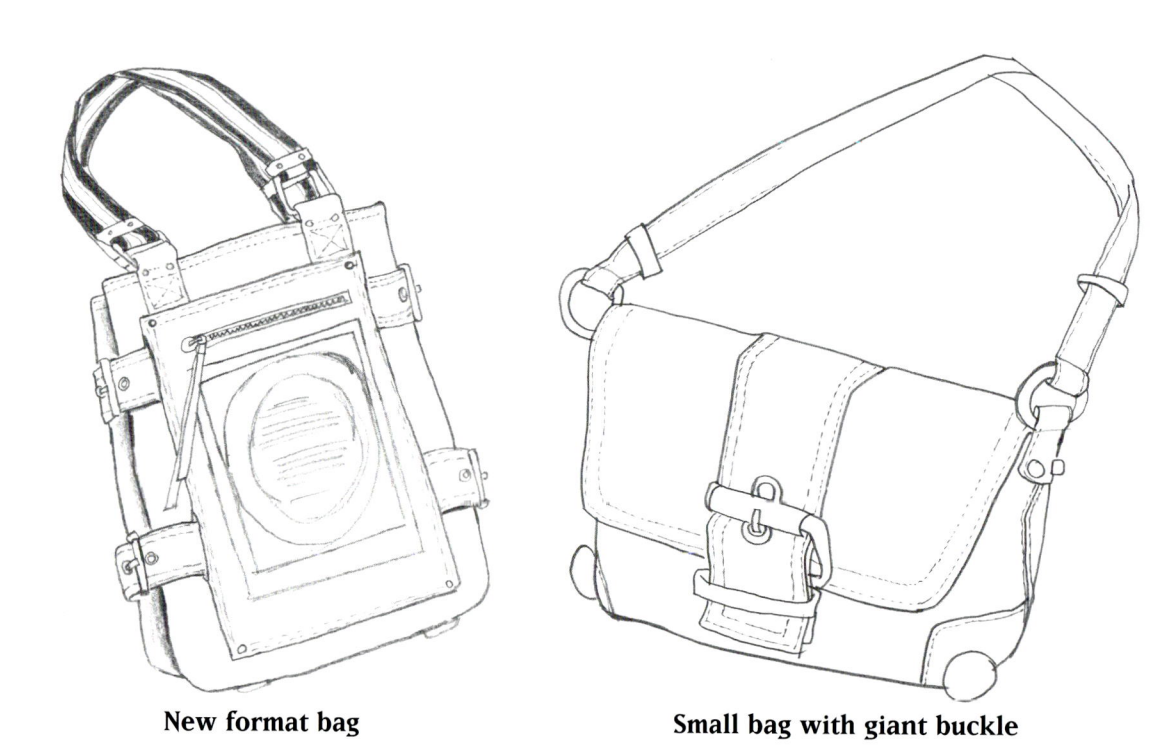

New format bag

Small bag with giant buckle

Bag with leather bottom and trimmings

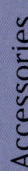

Purse

Padded bag

Bag/briefcase with compartments

Accessories

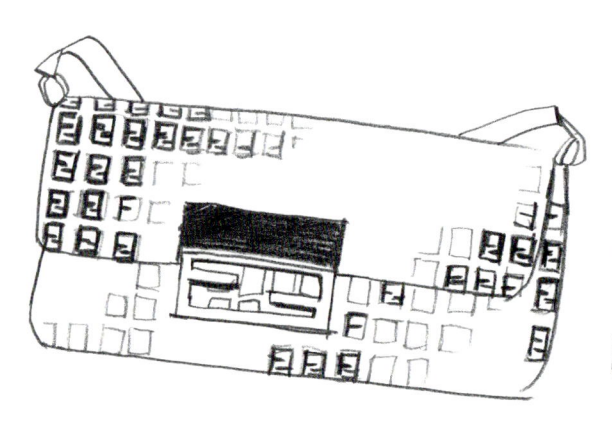

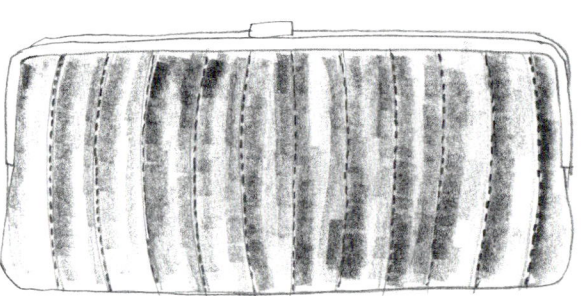

Baguette bag

Padded purse

Retro bag

Classic bag

Accessories

Beaded purse with feathers

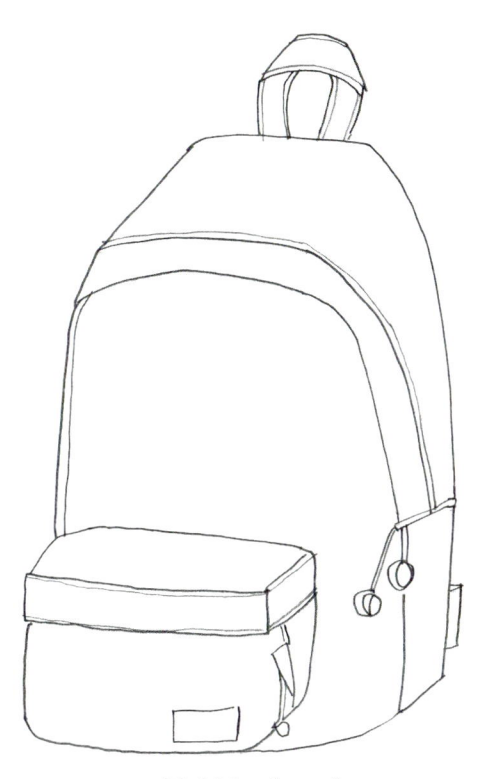

Rigid backpack

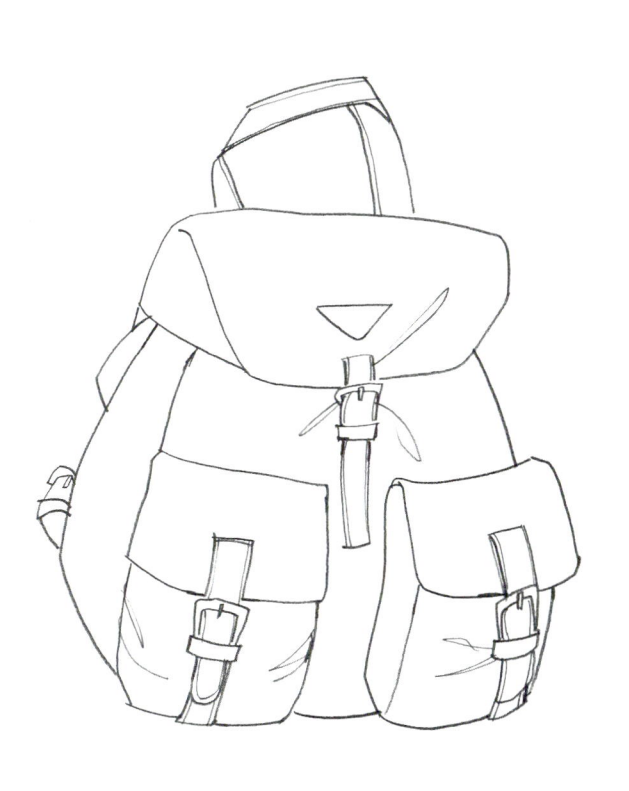

Soft backpack

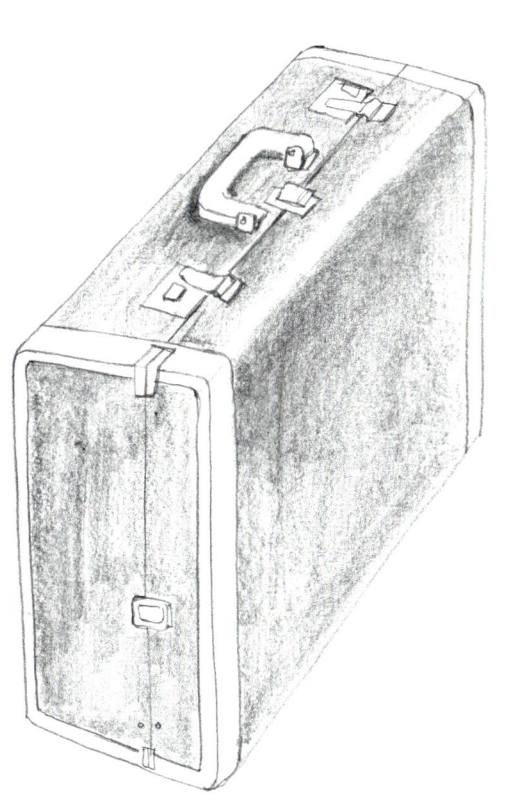

Rigid suitcase

Accessories

Soft laptop case

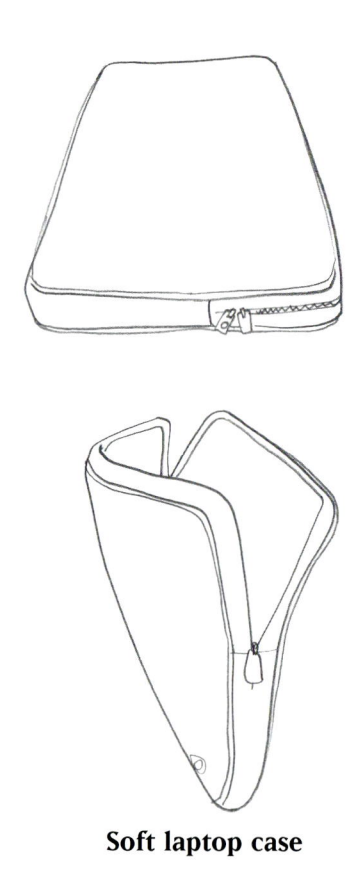

Executive laptop bag

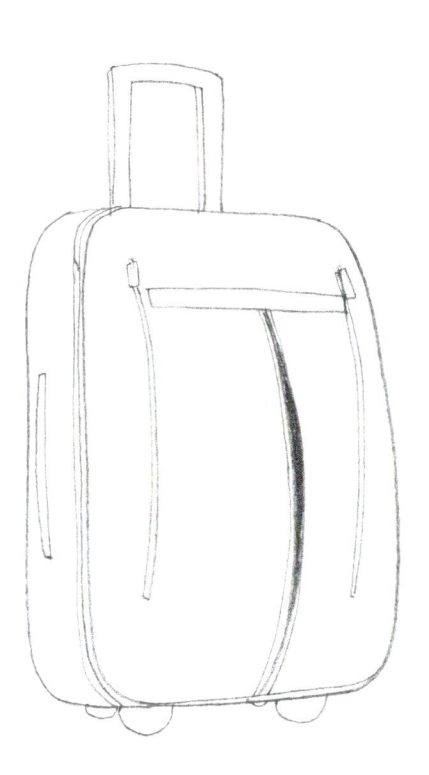

Suitcase with wheels

Multi-zip travel bag

Accessories

124

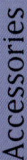

Bag with front pocket

Laptop bag

Sports bag

Knitted bag with rigid handle

Accessories

125

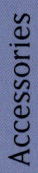

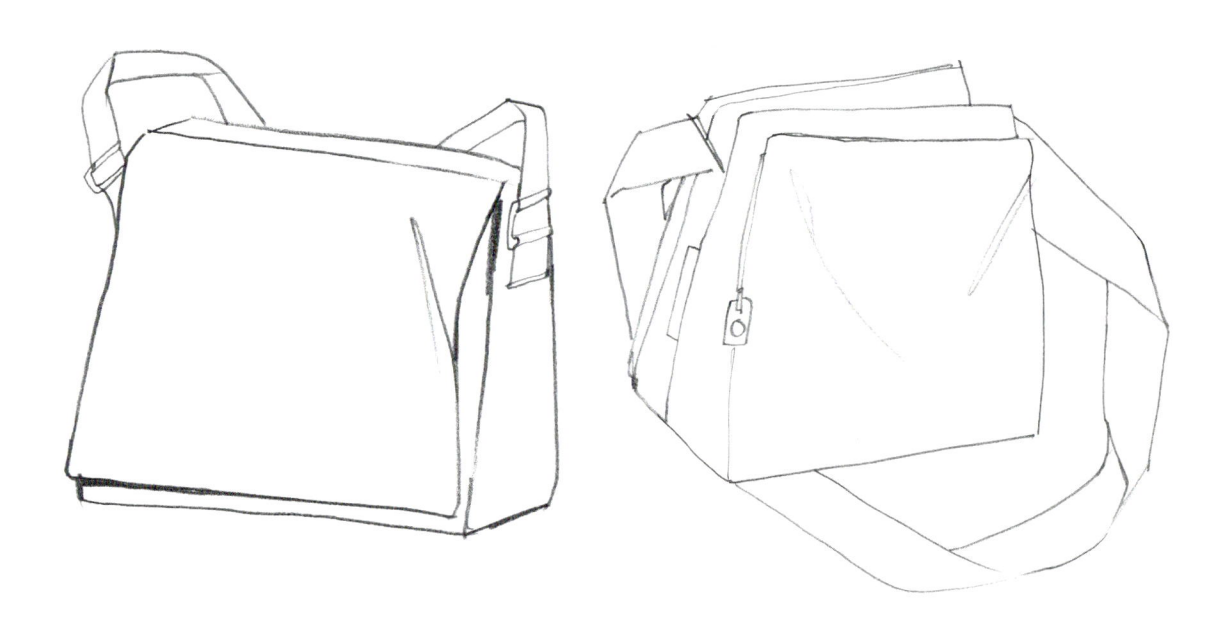

Bag with lapel

Nylon bag

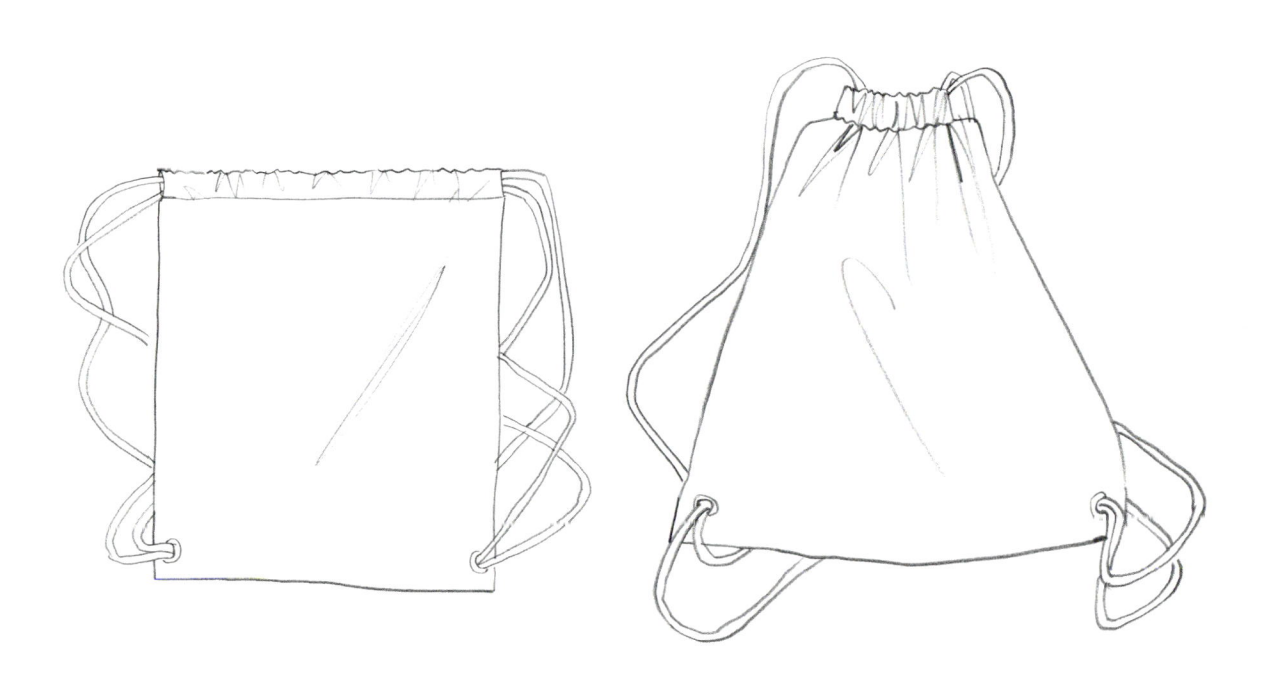

Nylon bag (open and closed)

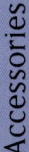

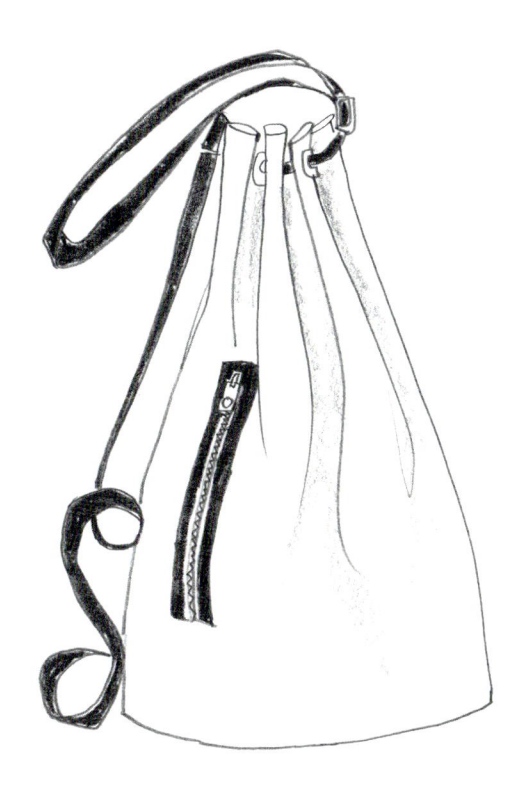

Soft bag

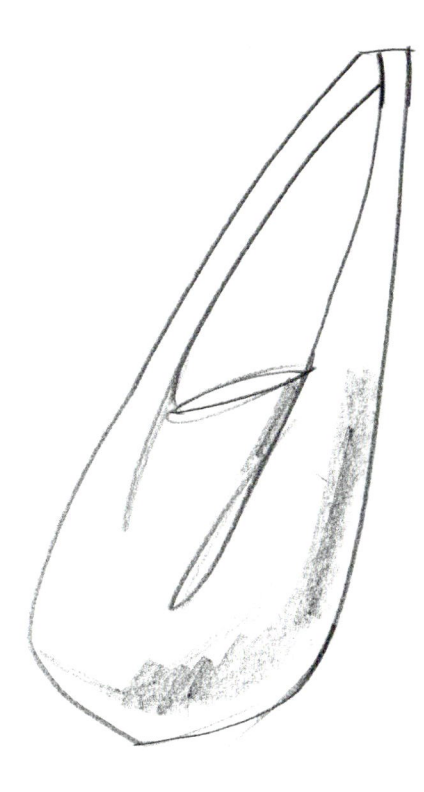

Bag

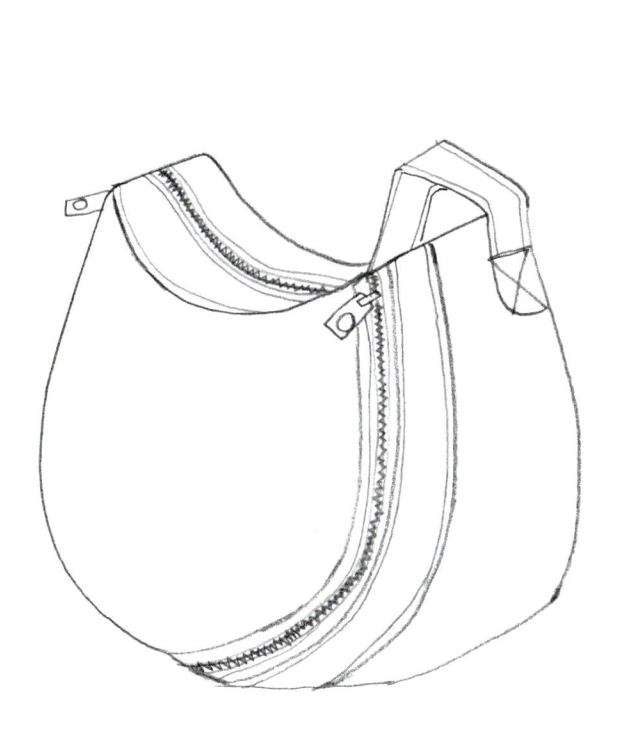

Leather bags

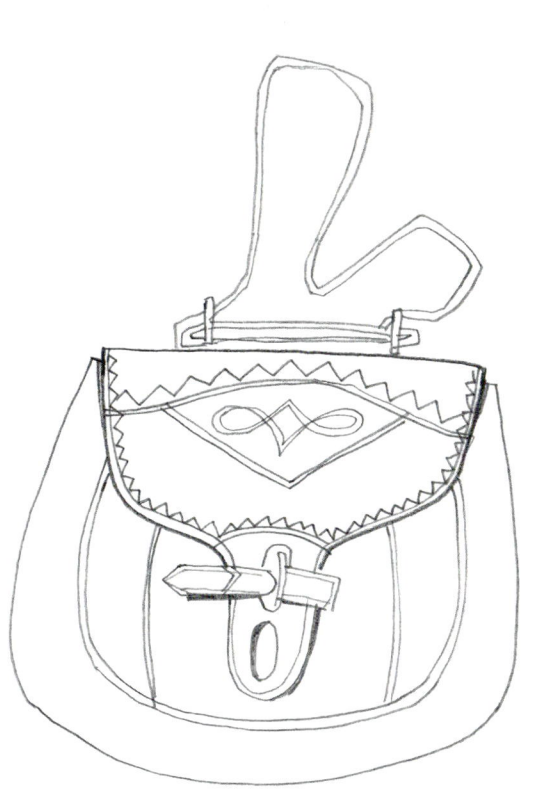

Accessories

Glam sunglasses

1980s style sunglasses

Aviator sunglasses

Horn-rimmed sunglasses

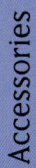

1970s style sunglasses

Lolita sunglasses  **1960s style sunglasses**

Accessories

Ear muffs

Knitted hat

Beret

Headbands

Accessories

Basic belts

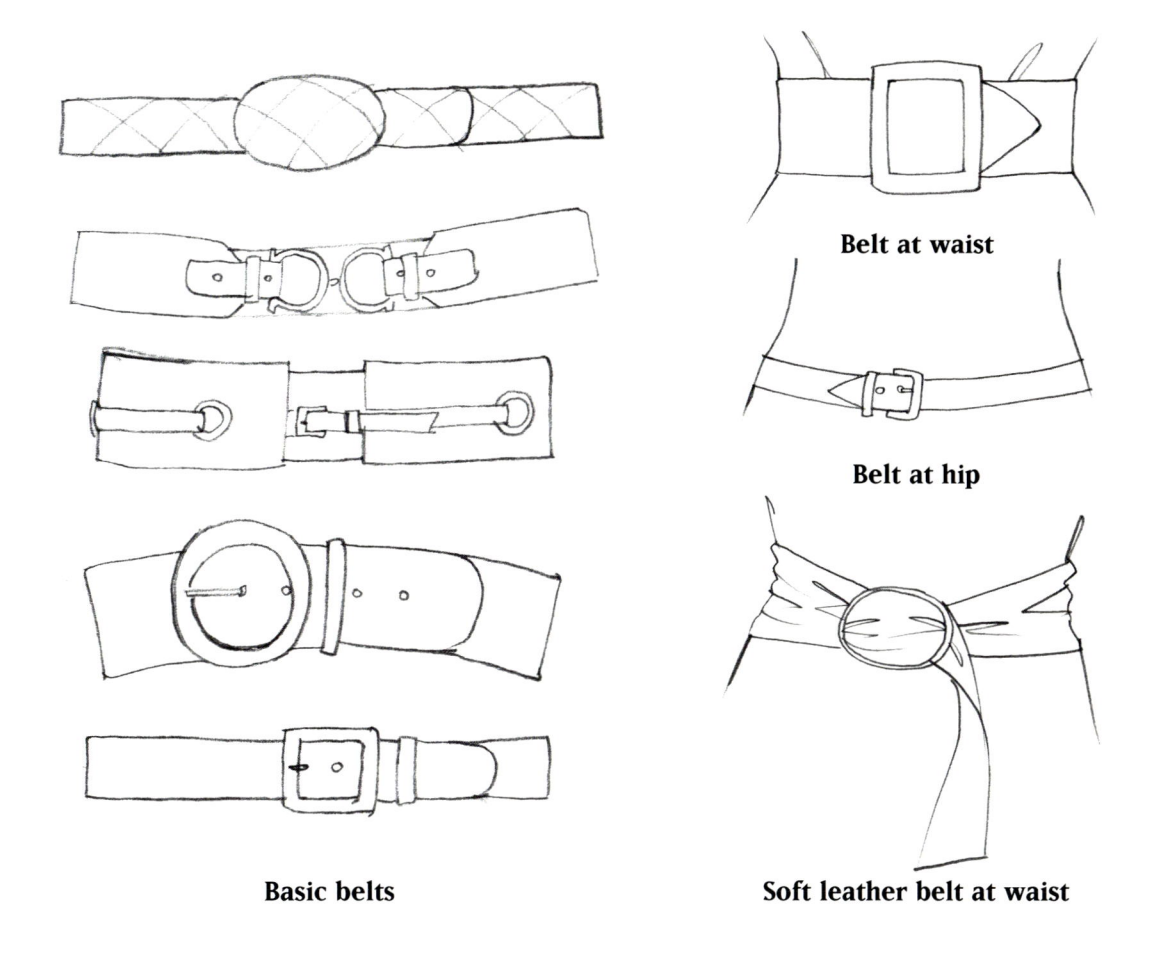

Belt at waist

Belt at hip

Soft leather belt at waist

Accessories

Cowboy hat

Broad-brimmed hat with flower

Top hat

Hat with scarf

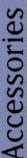

Boy's cap

1970s style cap

Scarves (front and profile)

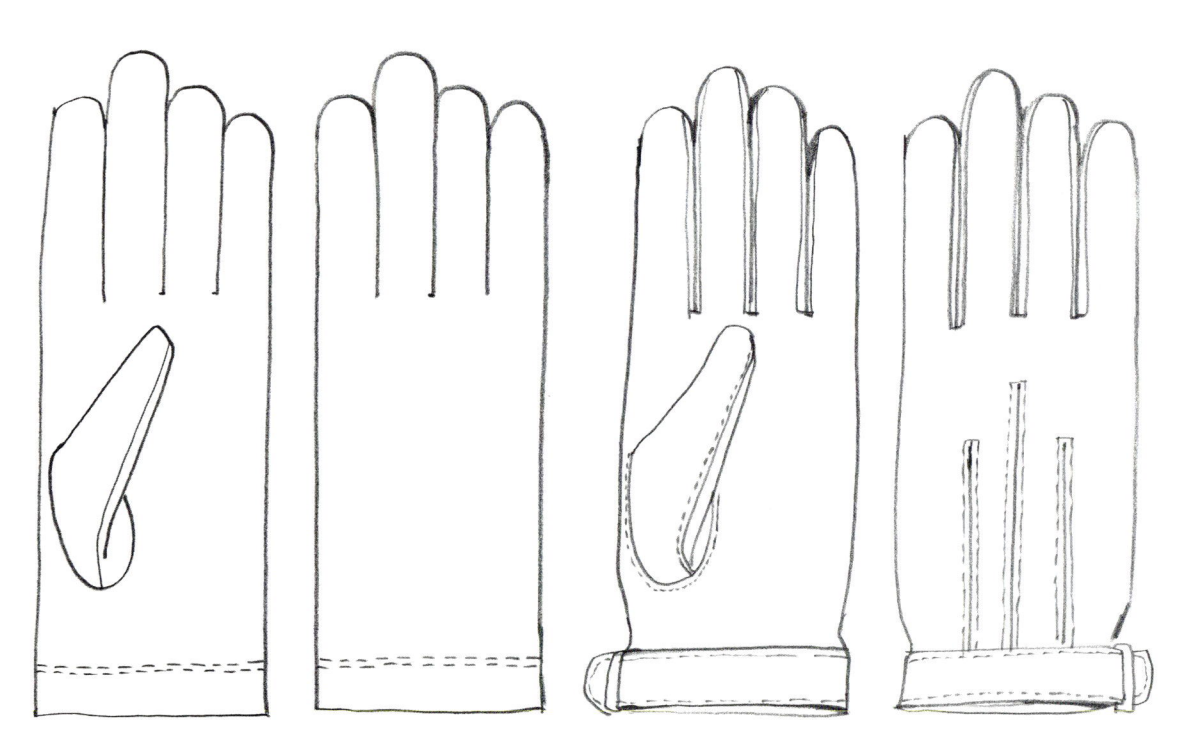

Classic gloves

Classic leather gloves

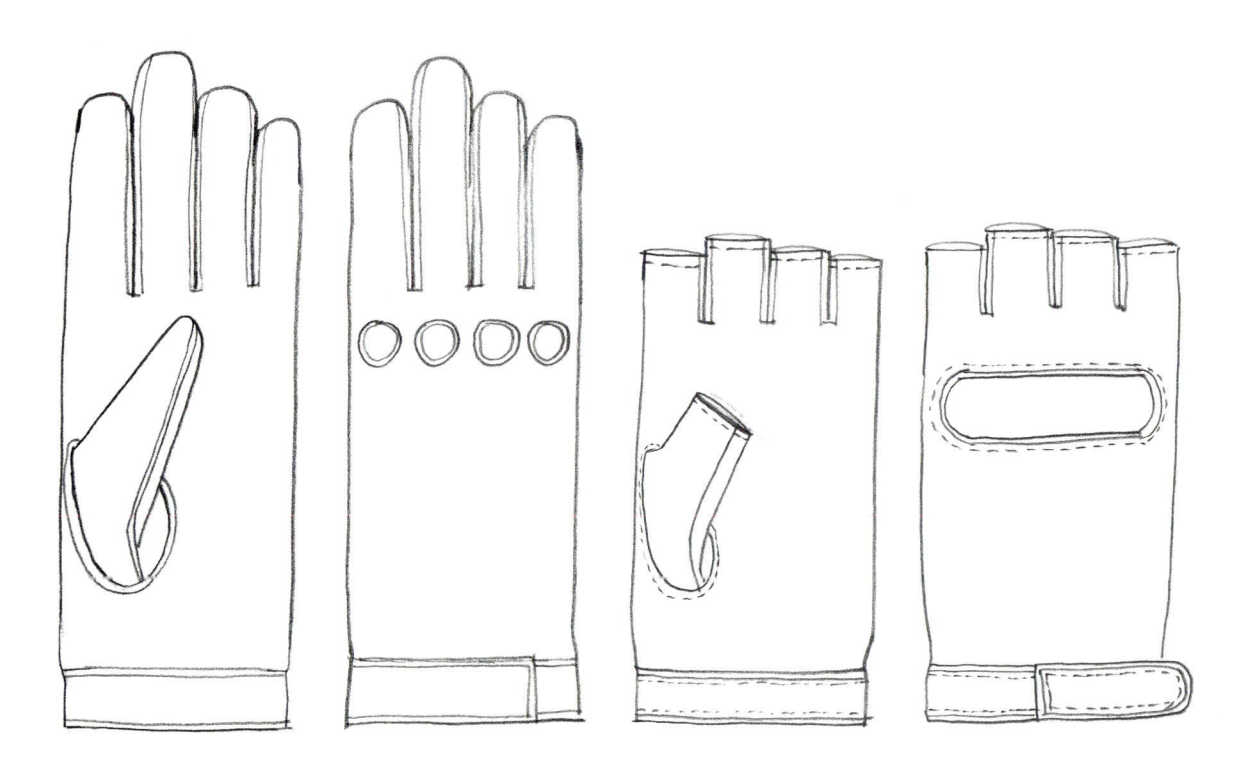

Gloves with perforated Velcro

Mitts

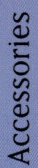

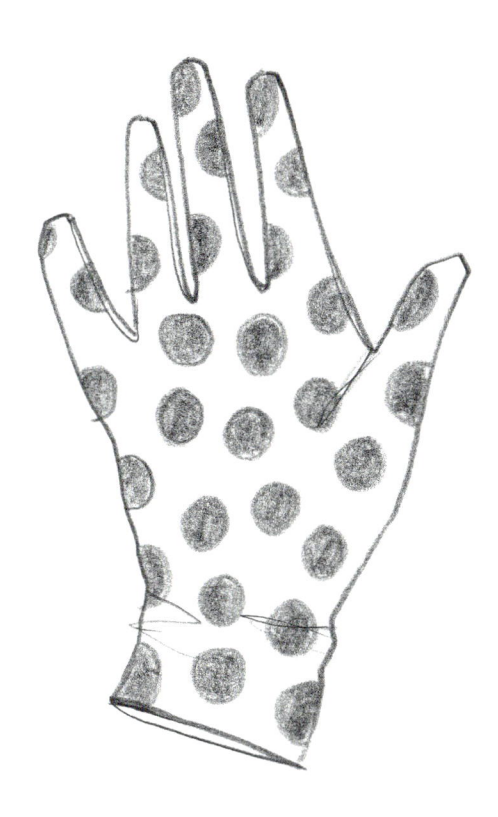

Print gloves

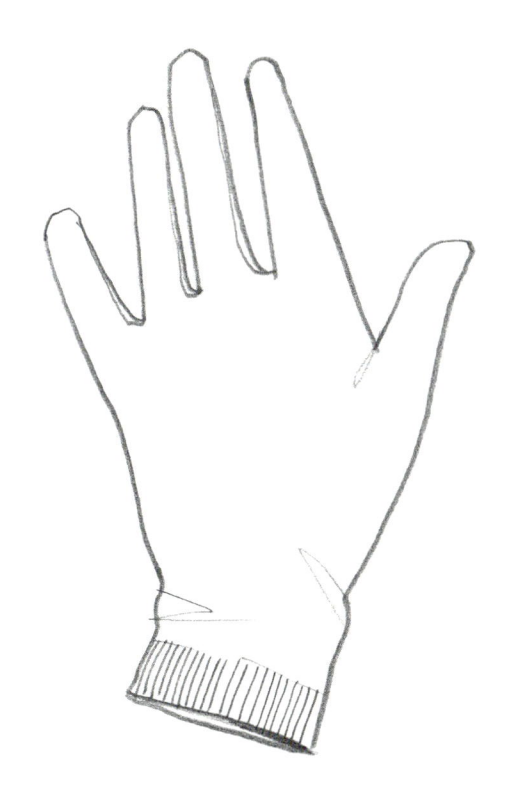

Plain gloves

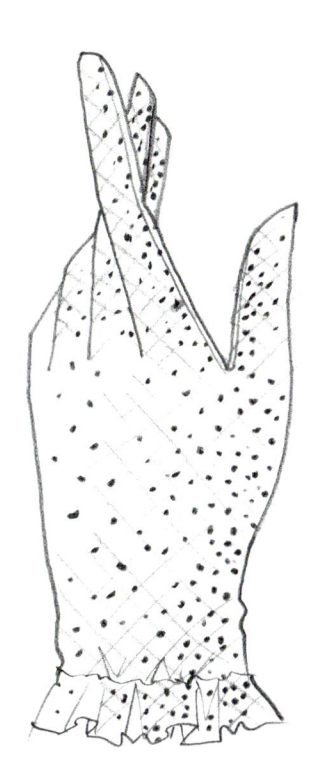

Lace gloves

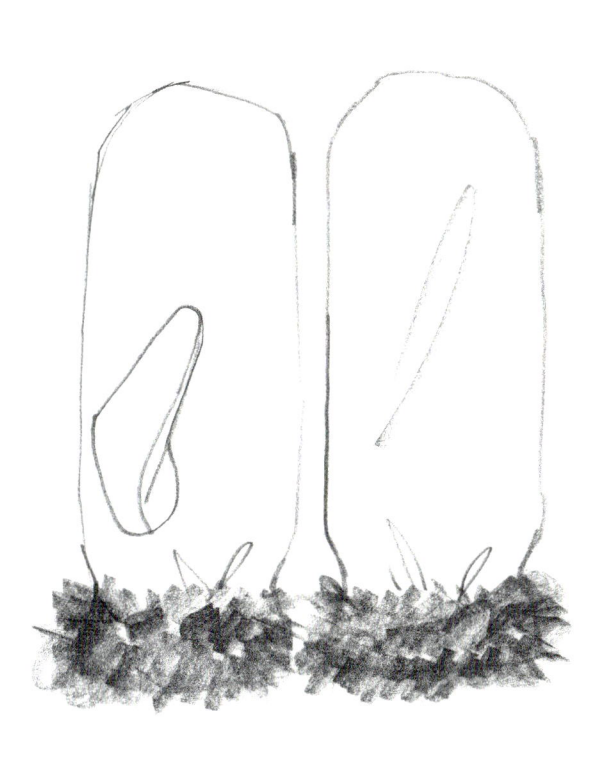

Mittens

Accessories

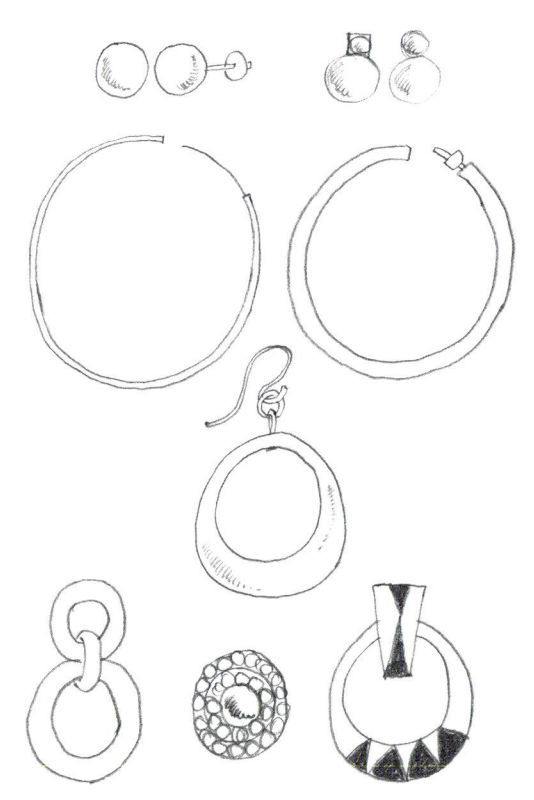

Hoops and round earrings

Earrings

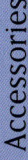

Basic rings

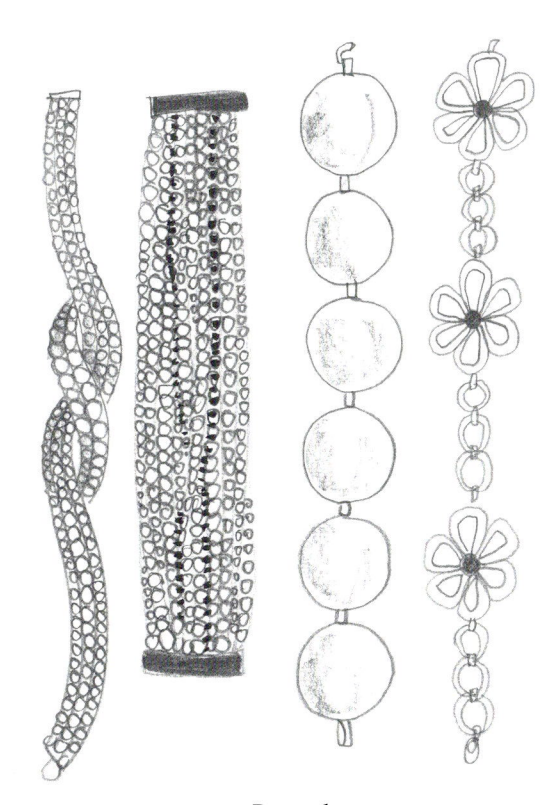

Bracelets

Accessories

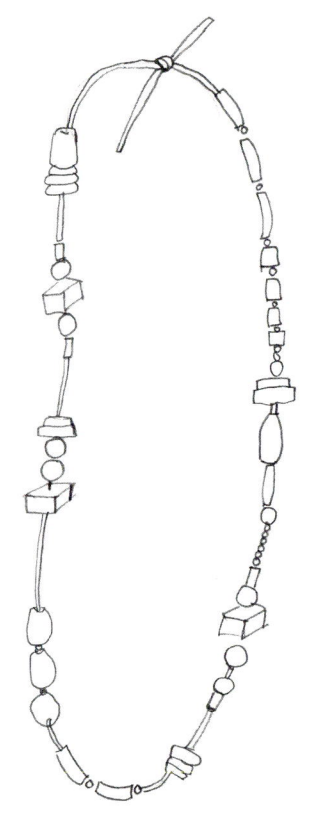

Wooden bead necklace

Metal pendant

Accessories

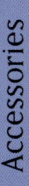

Necklace combining flowers, crochet work, pompon and wood

Chinese-inspired glass medallion belt

Accessories

Ready-to-wear details

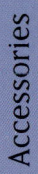

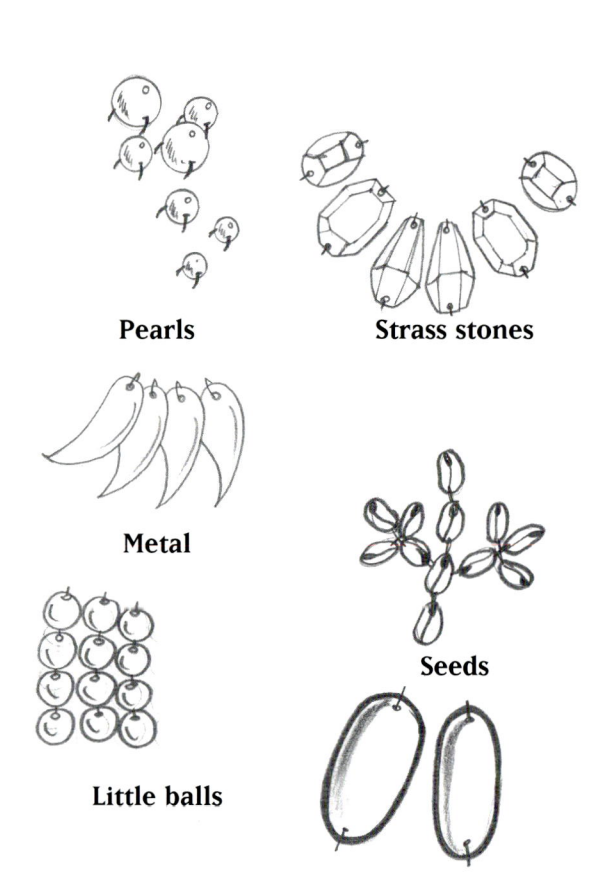

Pearls **Strass stones**

Metal

Little balls **Seeds**

Plastic

Accessories

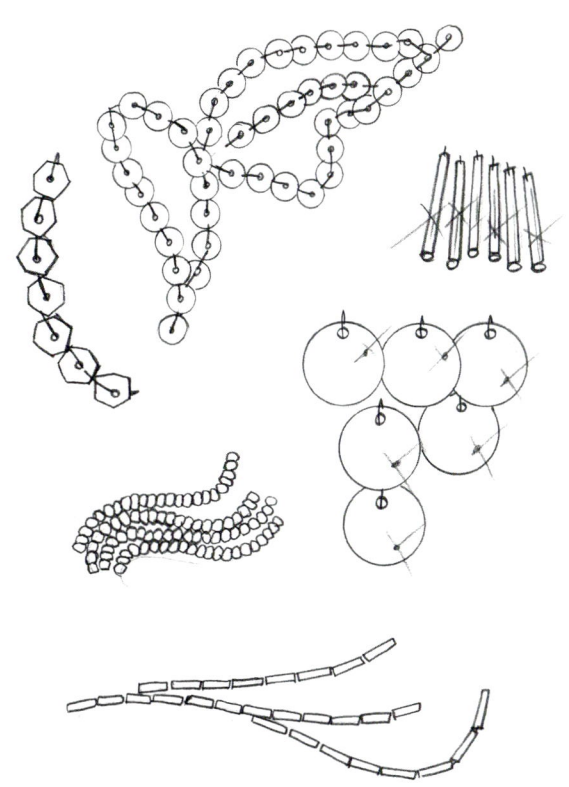

Embroidery: sequins and cannetille

Brooches

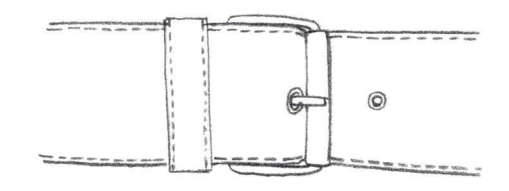

Square buckle

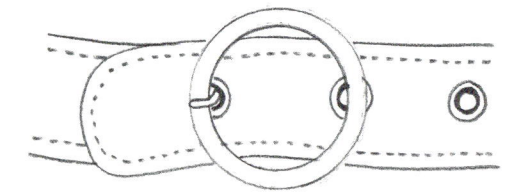

Round buckle

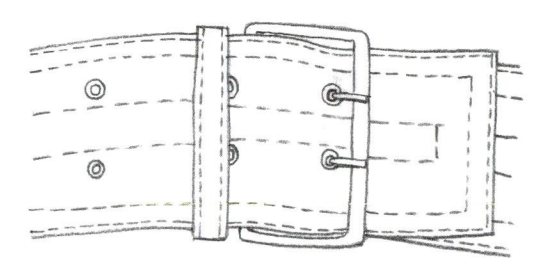

Double buckle

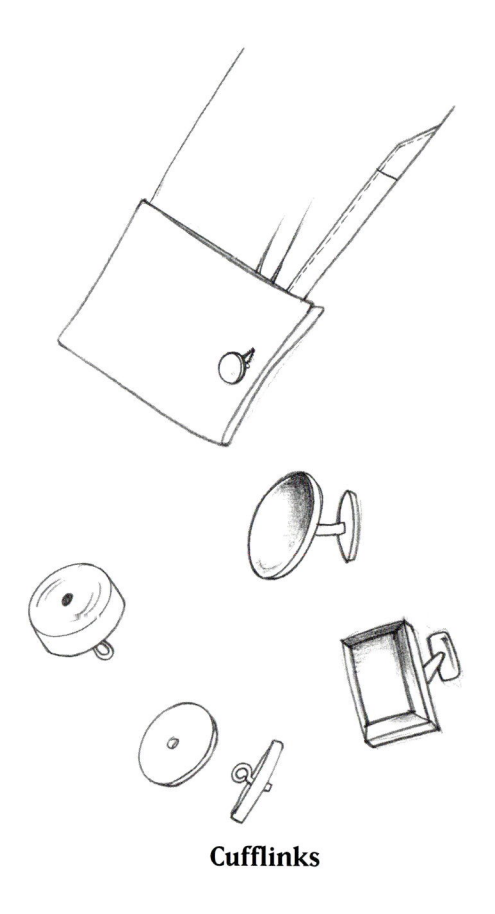

Cufflinks

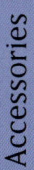

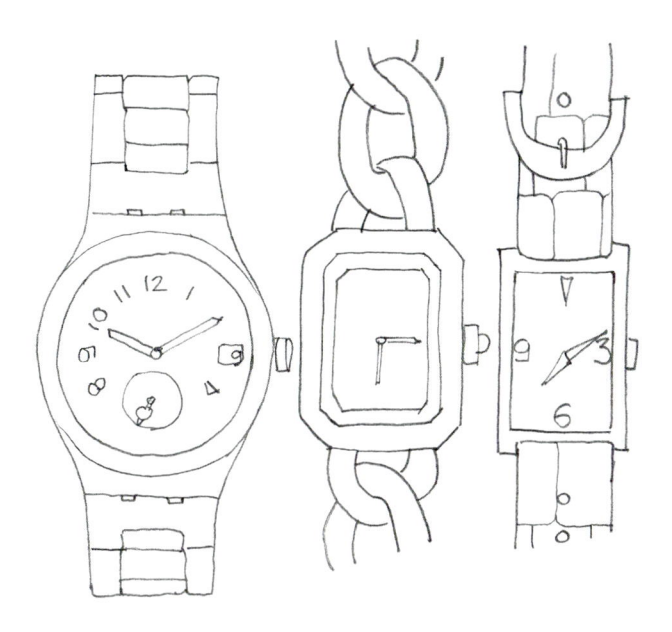

Base of watch (metal)   **Base of watch (chain)**   **Base of watch (leather)**

Drawing material

Accessories

143

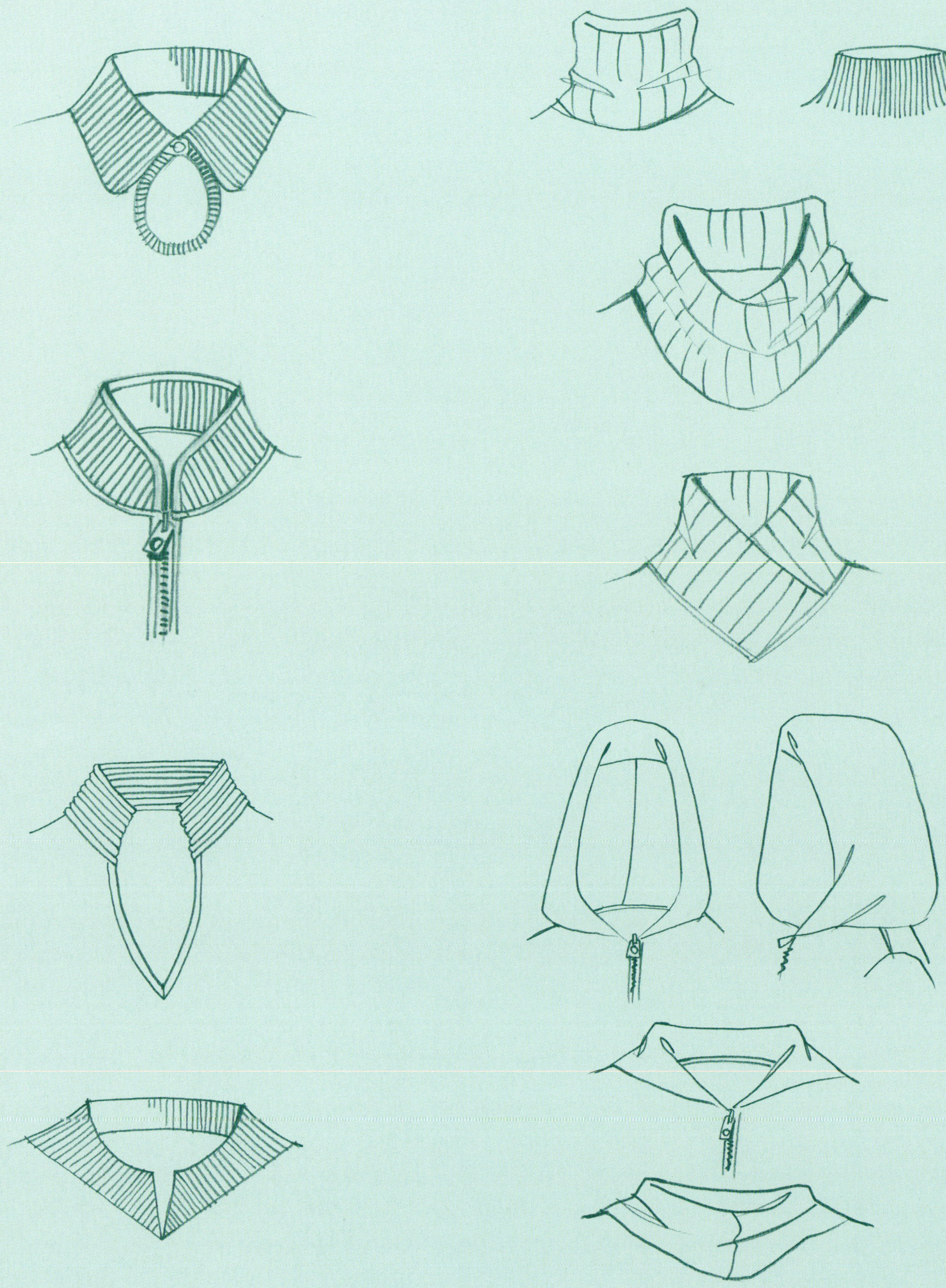

Details

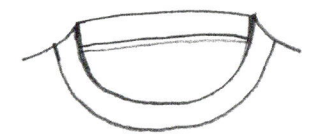

Crew neckline

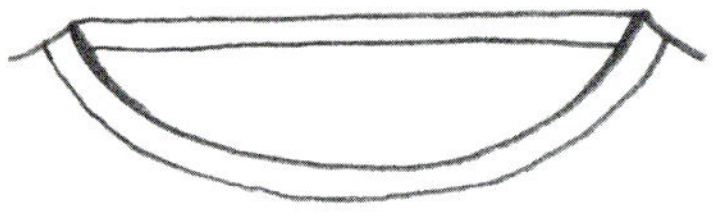

Scoop neckline

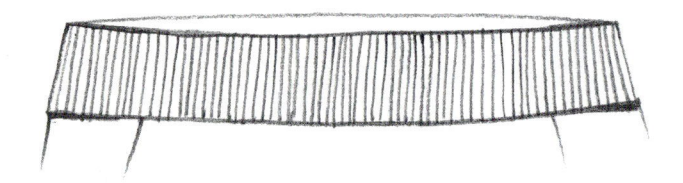

Very low scoop neckline

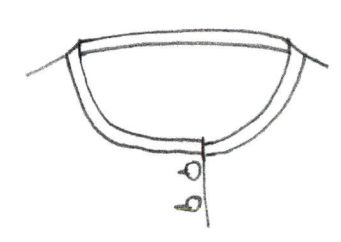

Bakers neckline

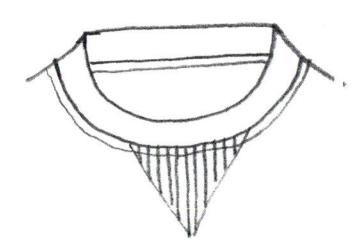

Sweatshirt neckline

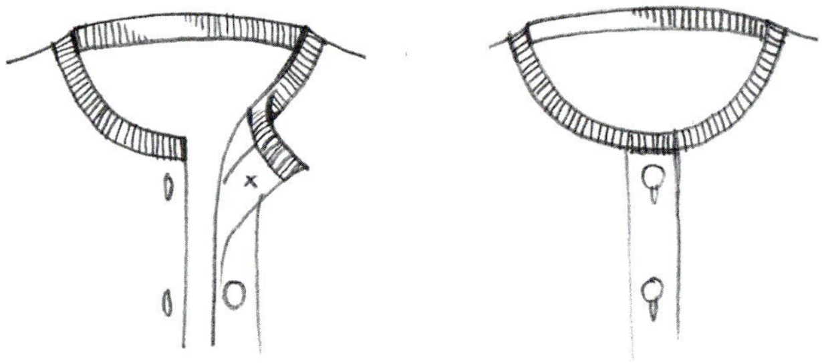

Classic cardigan neckline

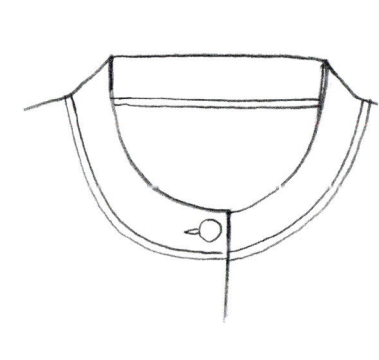

Crew neck jacket neckline

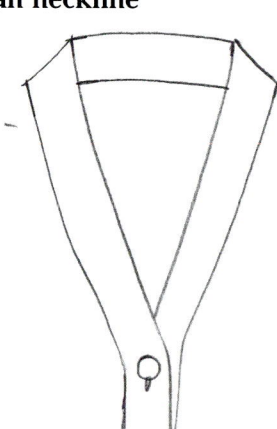

Cardigan jacket neckline

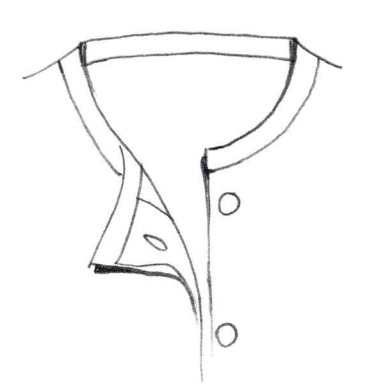

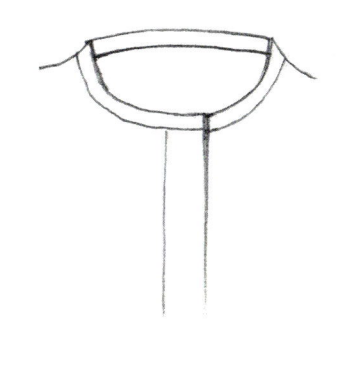

Jacket collar with inside strip

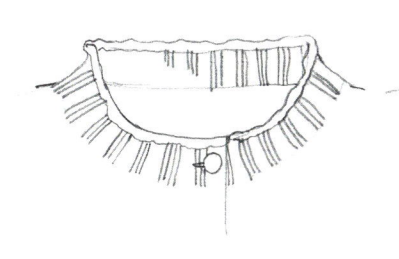

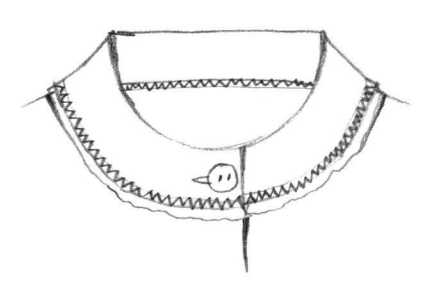

Jacket collar with kink finishing

Jacket collar applied to the garment with covered seams

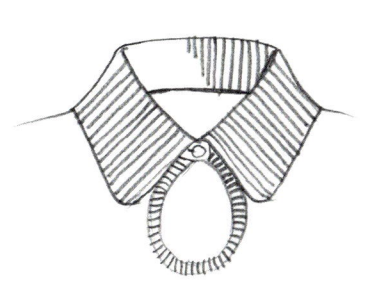

Shirt neckline with tear

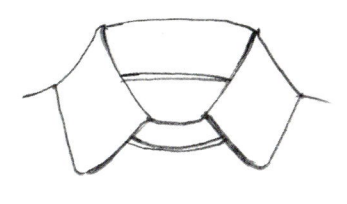

Closed shirt neckline

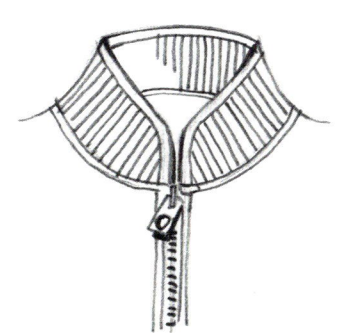

Mao neckline with zip

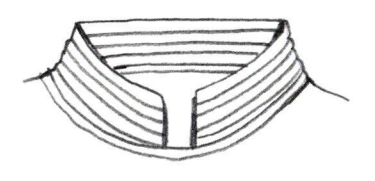

Mao shirt neckline with bourrelets

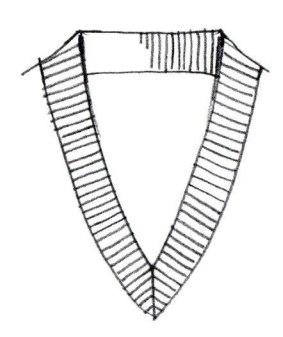

Classic V neck

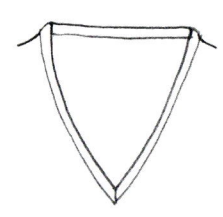

Closed V neck

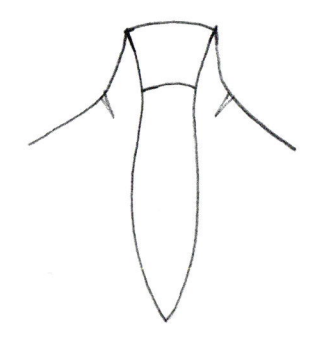

Retro V neck

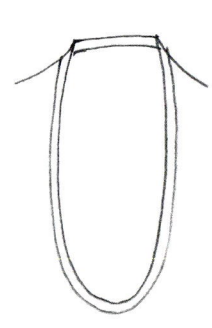

Deep and rounded V neck

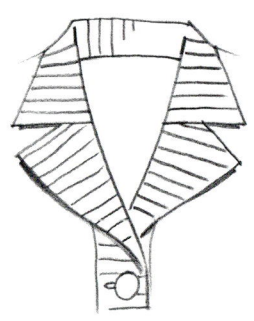

Jacket collar with ribbed lapel

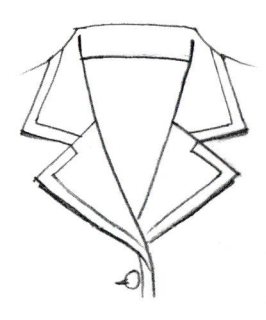

Jacket collar with tubular lapel

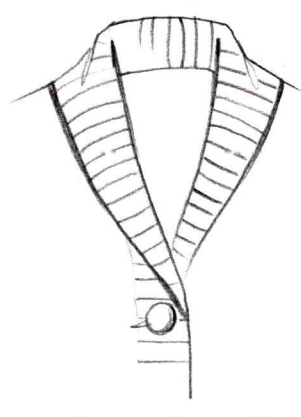

Smocking jacket collar

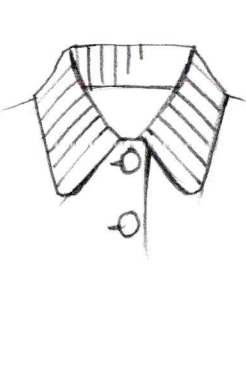

Shirt jacket collar

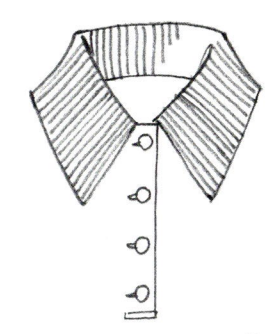

Classic polo shirt collar

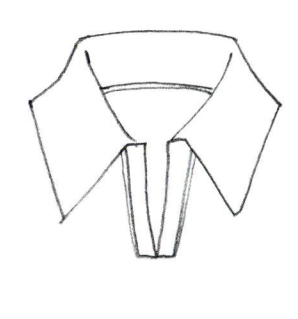

Polo shirt collar without buttons

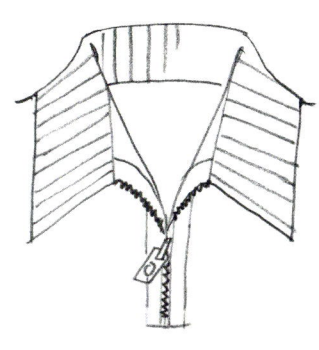

Polo shirt collar with zip

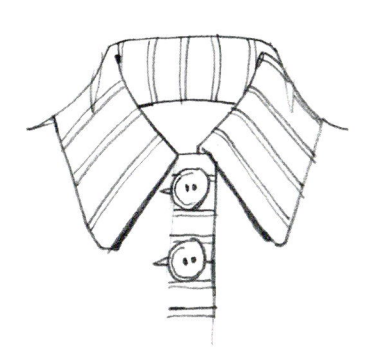

Thick knit polo shirt collar

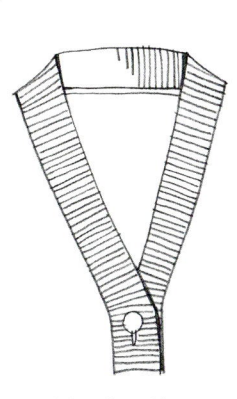

Ribbed collar

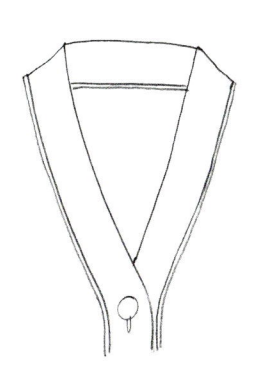

Flat collar

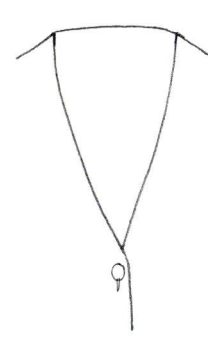

Machine collar

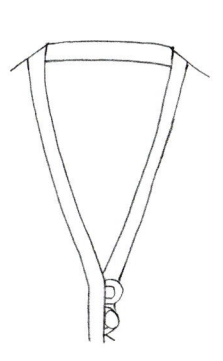

Tubular collar with bar tacks

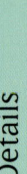

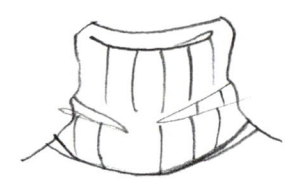

Classic turtleneck

Semi-turtleneck

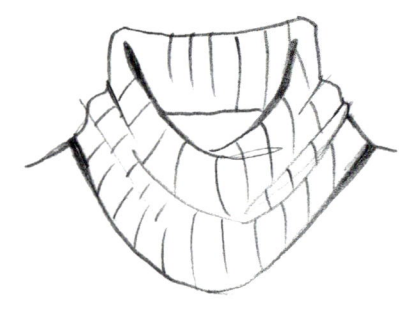

Loose turtleneck

Crossed turtleneck

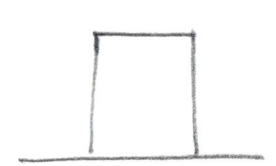

How not to draw a turtleneck

How to draw a turtleneck: draw the curved line

How not to draw a turtleneck

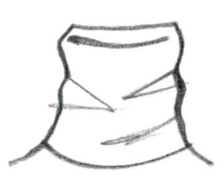

How to draw a turtleneck: lines come out from the sides

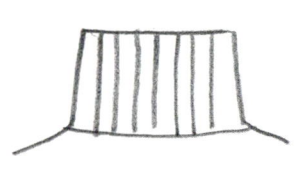

How not to draw a turtleneck

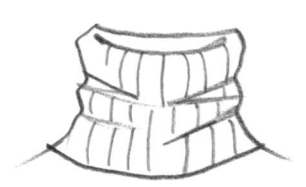

How to draw a turtleneck: follow the waves of the creases, giving curves to the ribbing

Details

150

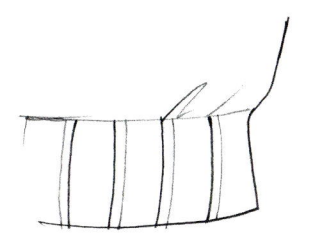

How to draw a thick sweater: with wider rib lines

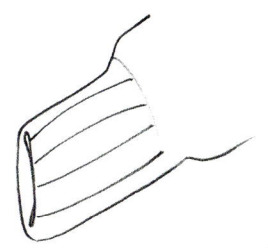

How to draw a thick sweater: with rounder and larger shapes

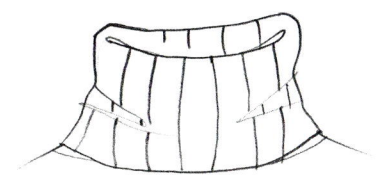

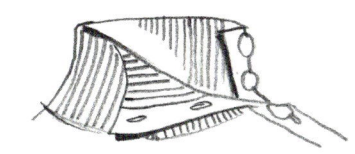

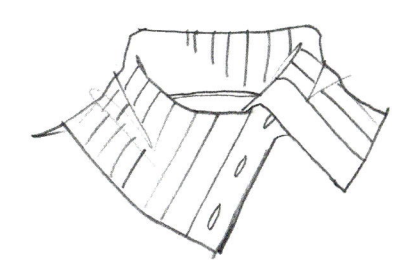

Turtleneck buttoned on one side

Turtleneck with zip

Details

Classic bow tie

Butterfly bow tie (1970s style)

Loop bow tie

Classic bow tie (1960s style)

Ceremonial bow tie

Satin bow

Gauze bow

Cobbler bow

Ribbon bow

Cord bow

Details

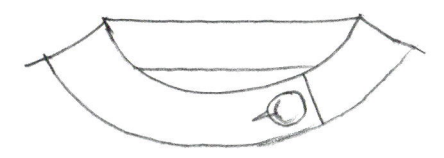

Crew collar fancy neckline with wide strip and button

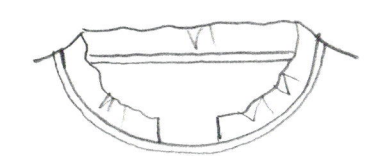

Fancy neckline with appliqué fabric

Knotted turtleneck fancy neckline

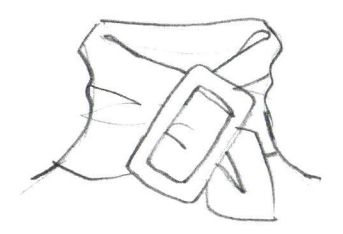

Turtleneck with fancy buckle neckline

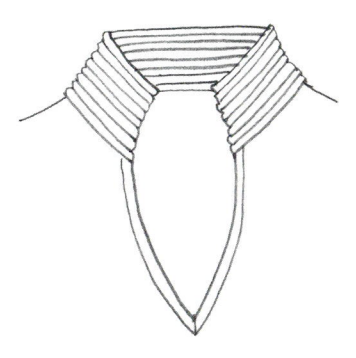

Fancy ribbed neckline with V neck

Fancy neckline with tuck

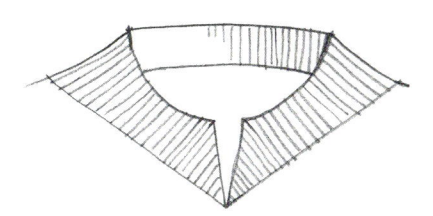

Fancy neckline with crew and open

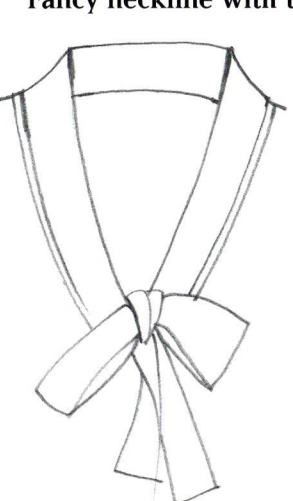

Fancy V neck with bow

Details

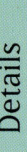

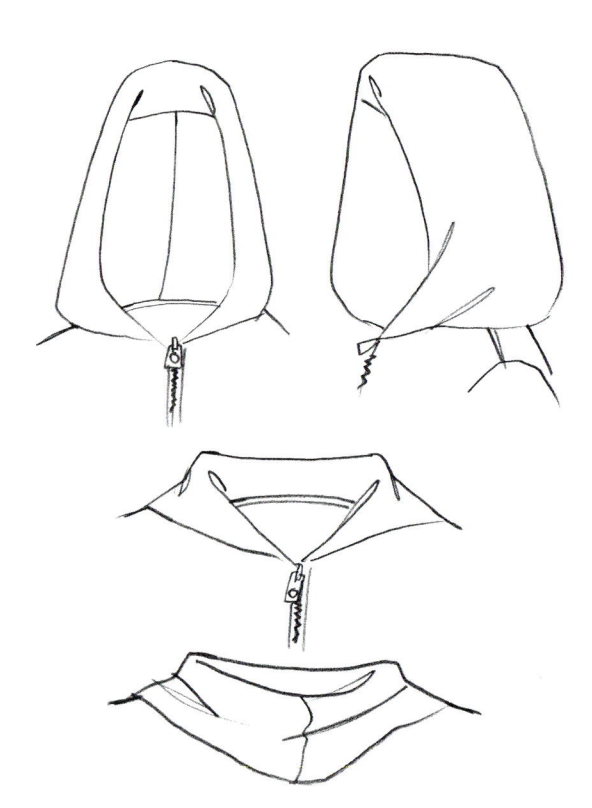

Hoods

Crossed tie with satin ribbon, bodice-style

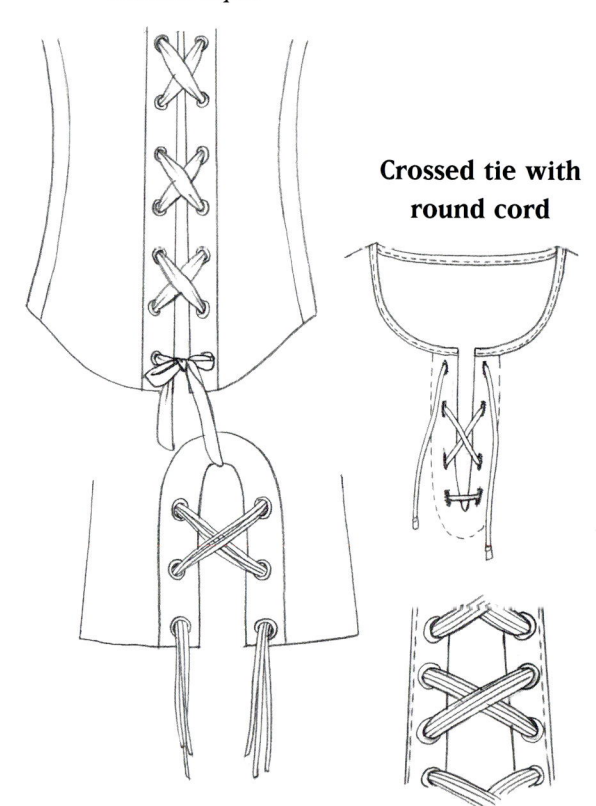

Crossed tie with round cord

Crossed tie with various suede strips

Overlapping crossed tie with flat cord (sports shoes)

Mini ribbing and crossed button-up tie

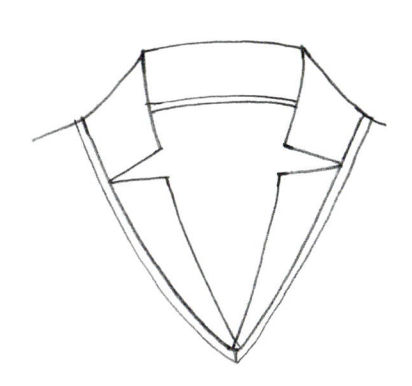

Fancy neckline with inverted lapel

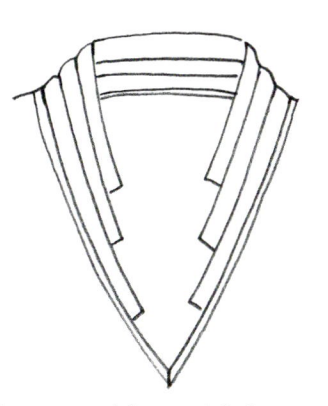

Fancy neckline with bourrelets

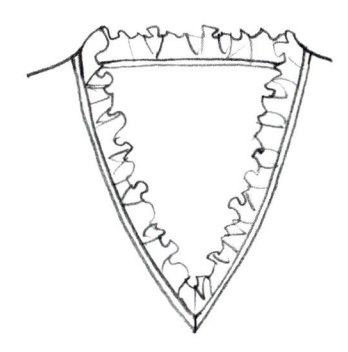

Fancy neckline with frills

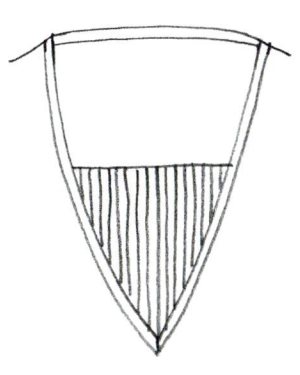

Fancy neckline ribbed piece enclosing the V neck

Details

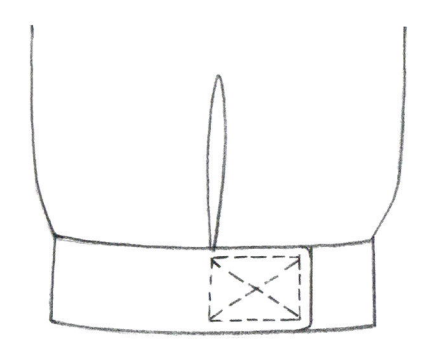

Velcro closed

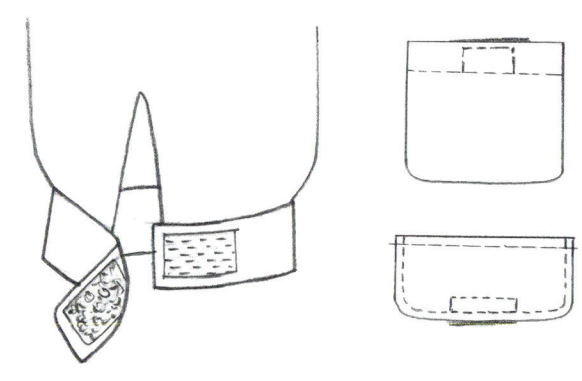

Velcro open

Velcro patches

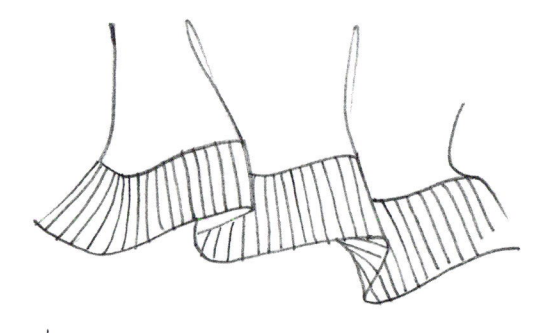

Garment basics: frills

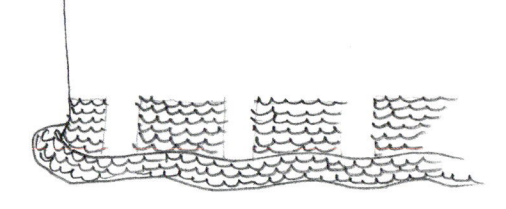

Garment basics: links

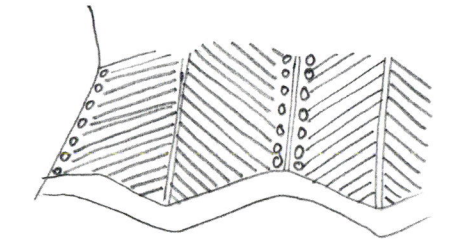

Garment basics: drawnwork

Details

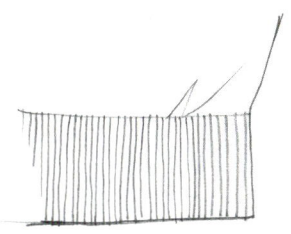

**How to draw a fine sweater:
with geometric and harder shapes**

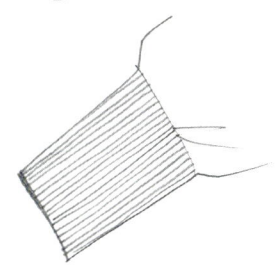

**How to draw a fine sweater:
with finer and closer rib lines**

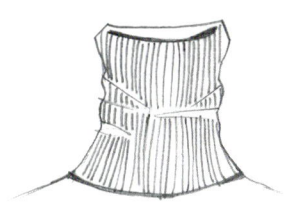

Feather details

Details

Garment basics: ribs (2 x 1)

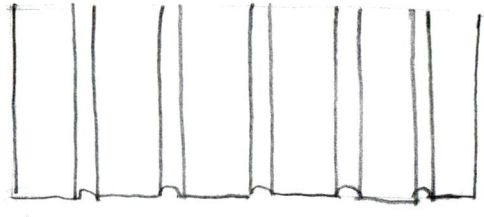

Garment basics: ribs (4 x 2)

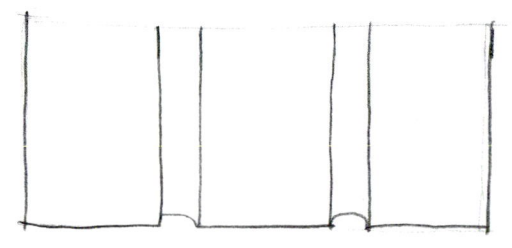

Garment basics: ribs (6 x 2)

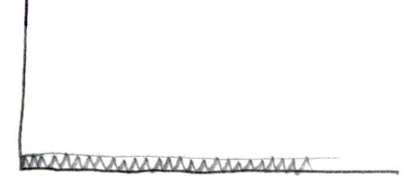

Garment basics: overlock stitch

Garment basics: double-needle stitch

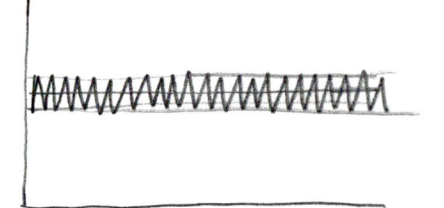

Garment basics: zig-zag stitch

Details

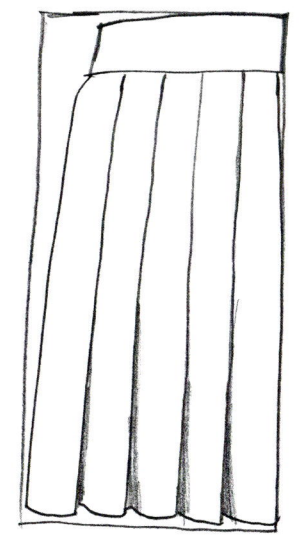

Pleats: 1. Draw with some shadow. Start half-way to give feeling of depth

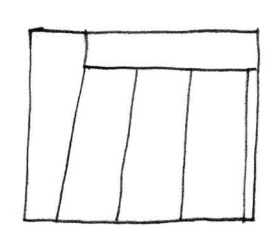

Pleats: 2. Distribute in shape of sun rays

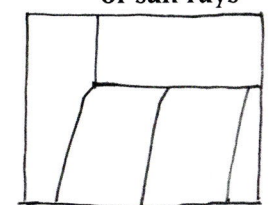

Pleats: 3. Curve line to give sense of thickness

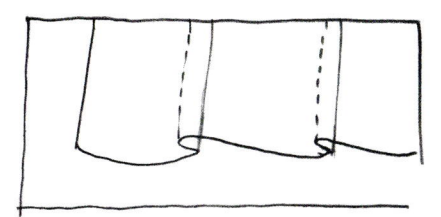

Pleats: 4. Curve line at bottom, move in and out to give sense of depth

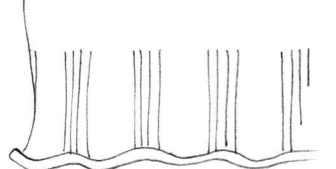

Garment basics: ribs with kink

Garment basics: wide tubular

Garment basics: unraveling

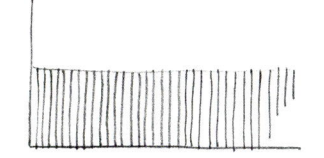

Garment basics: fine ribs

Details

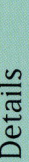

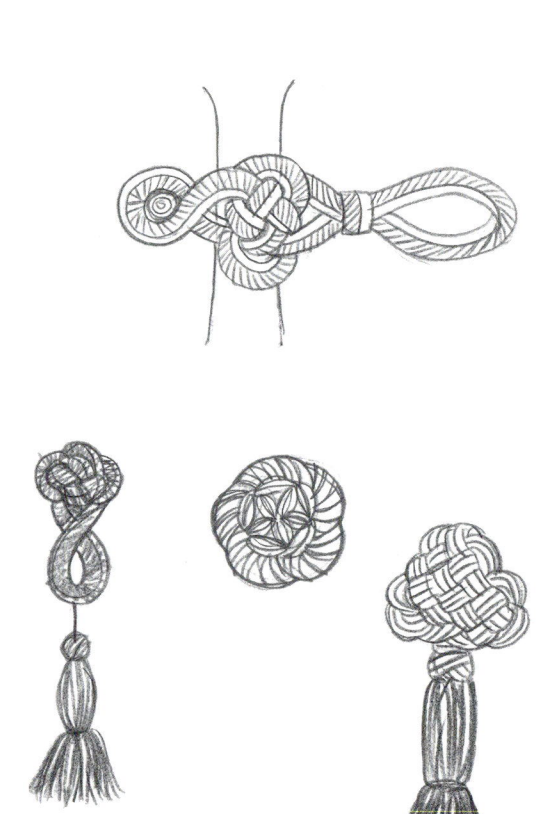

Trimmings: decorated buttons

Trimmings: decorated buttons

Details

Applications: embroidery and lace

Flower decorations

Details

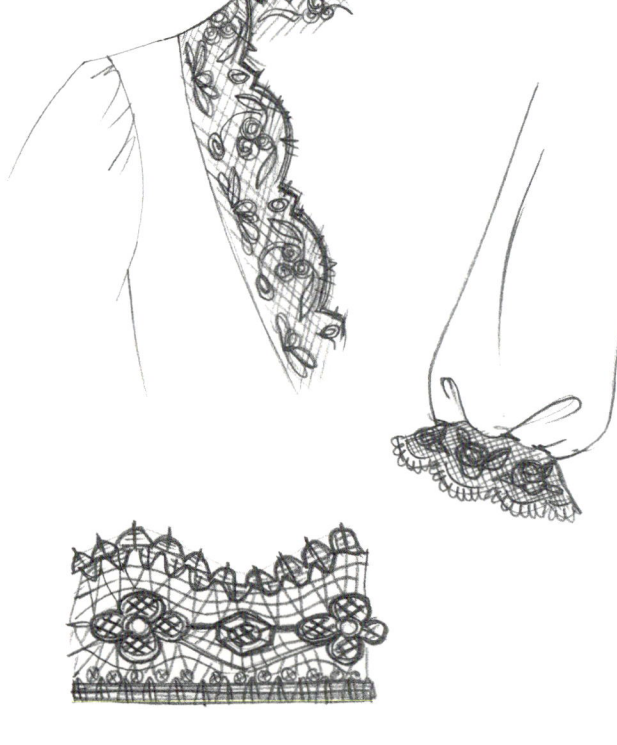

Applications: lace and silk lace

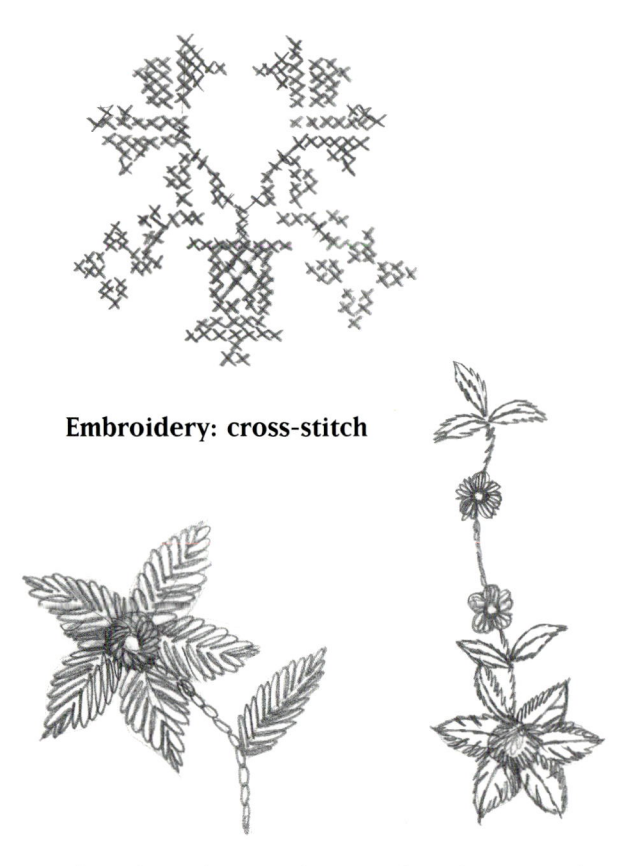

Embroidery: cross-stitch

Embroidery: big stitch   **Embroidery: machine-stitch**

Details

Embroidery: ribbon

Embroidery: ribbon and cord

Embroidery: chain

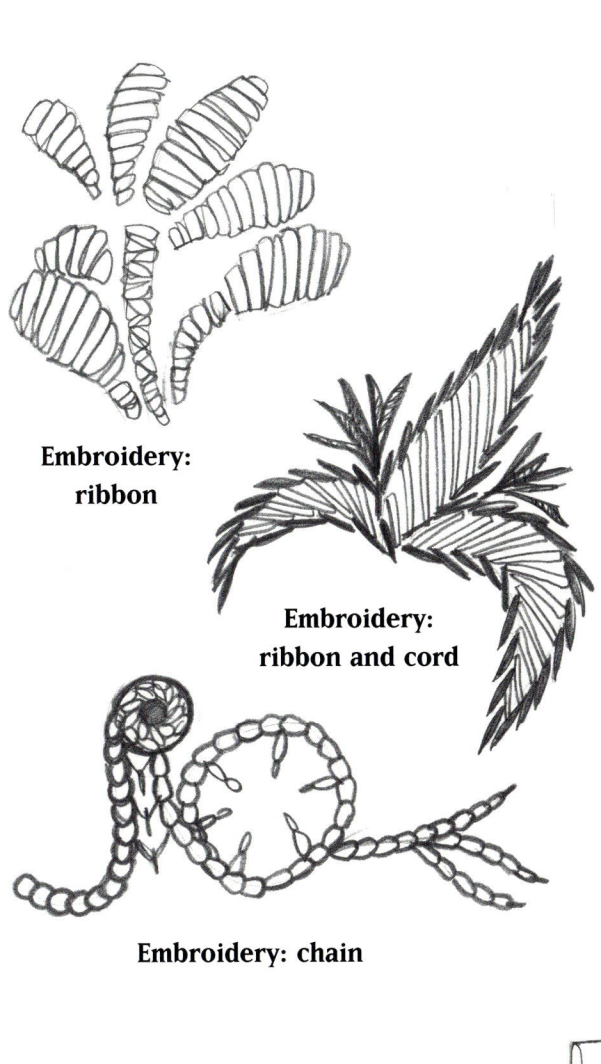

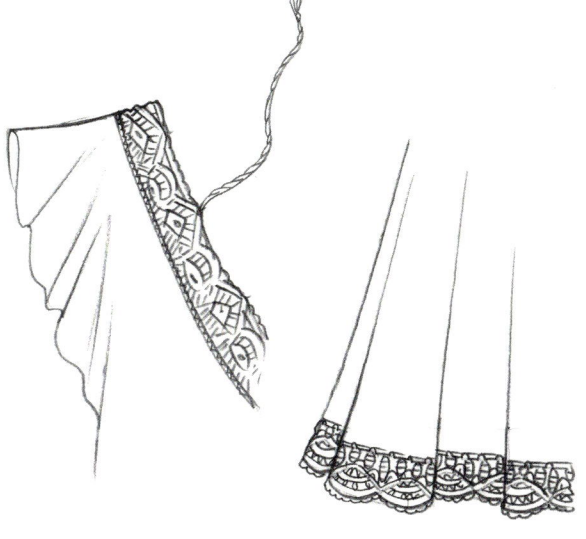

Applications: lace

Details

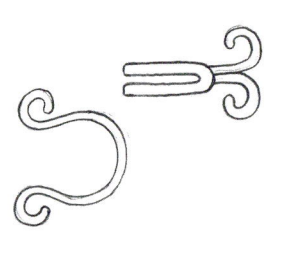

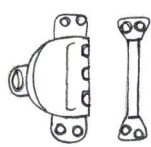

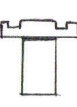

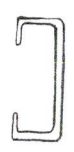

Brackets and eyelet

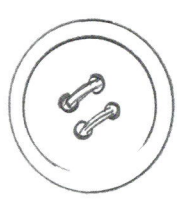

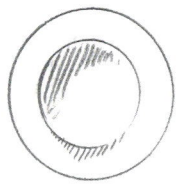

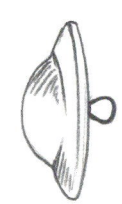

Flat button with 4 holes **Button with neck**

Details

164

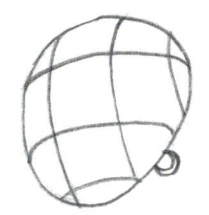

Leather button

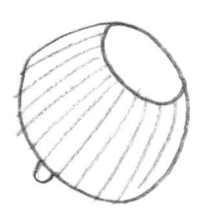

Retro button

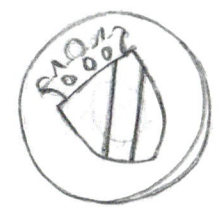

Blazer metal button

Intertwined cord button

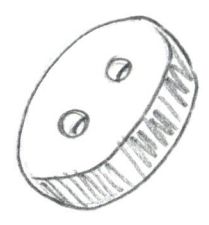

Horn button

Retro button

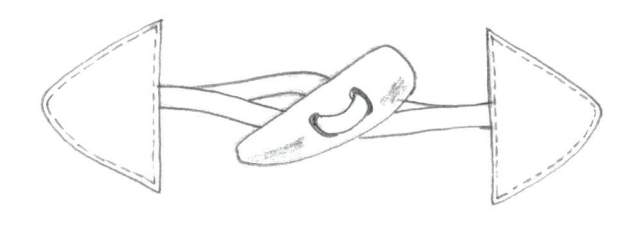

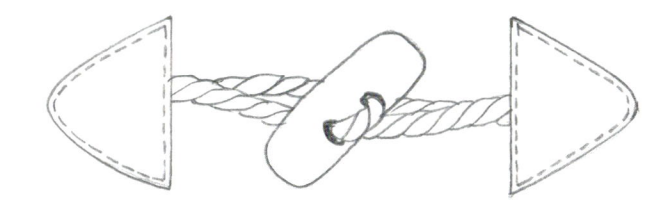

Fastener: classic horn

Fastener: metal

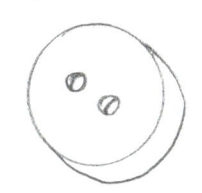

Fastener: round horn

Details

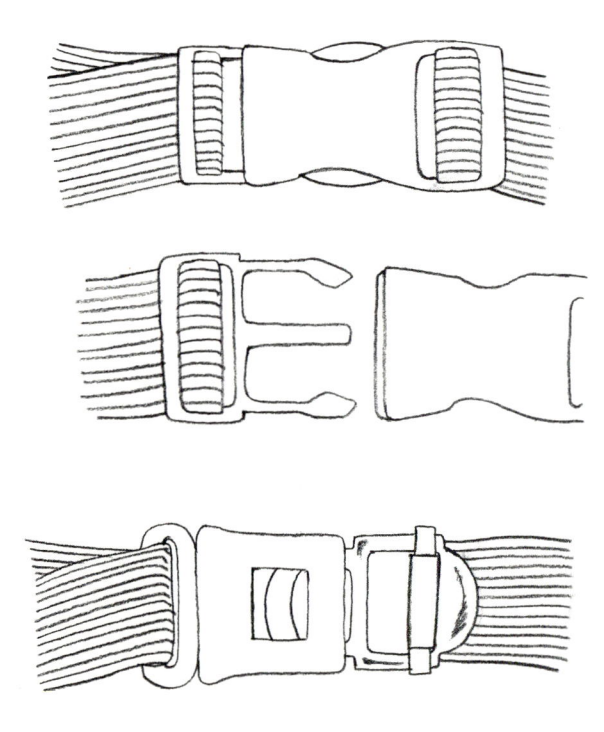

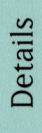

Plastic backpack fasteners

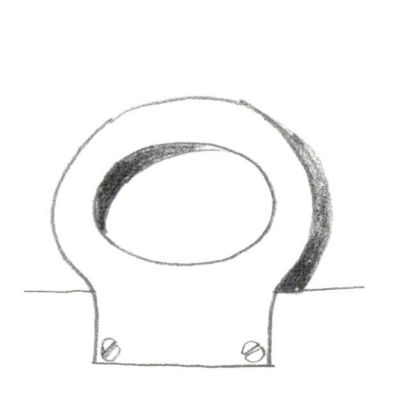

Flat/rigid handle

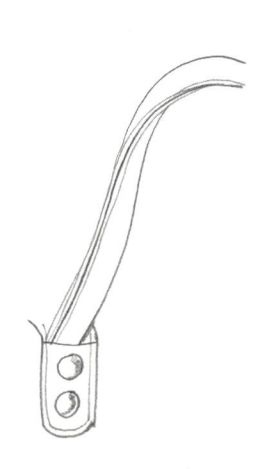

Round handle

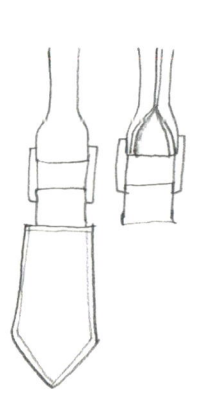

Handle with metal

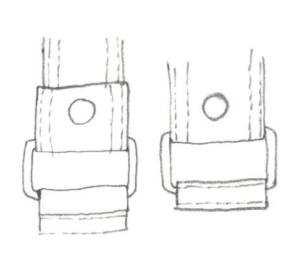

Flat sports handle

Classic metal zipper

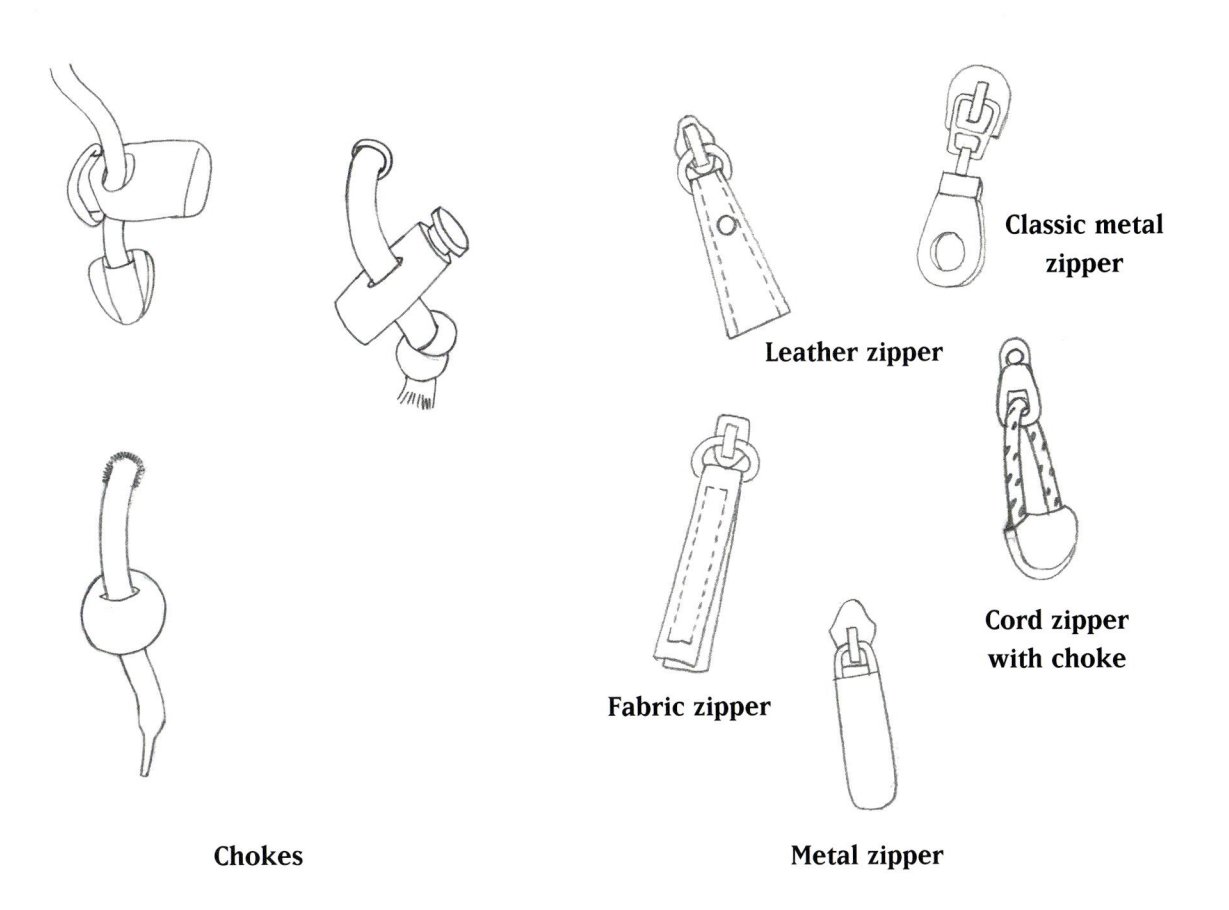

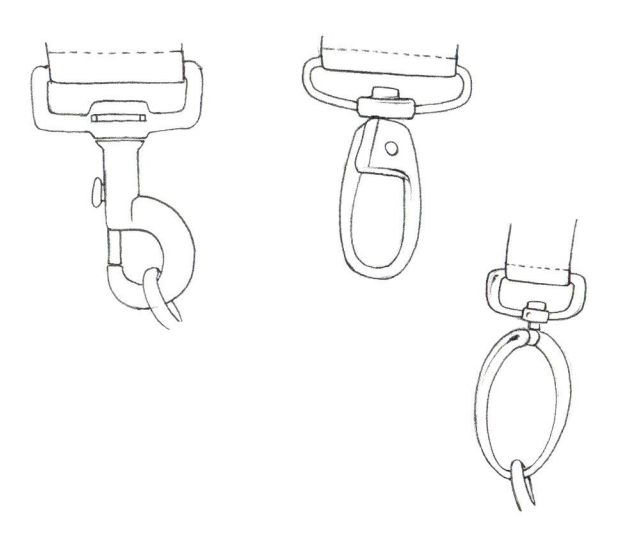

Leather zipper

Cord zipper with choke

Fabric zipper

Metal zipper

Chokes

Snap rings

Details

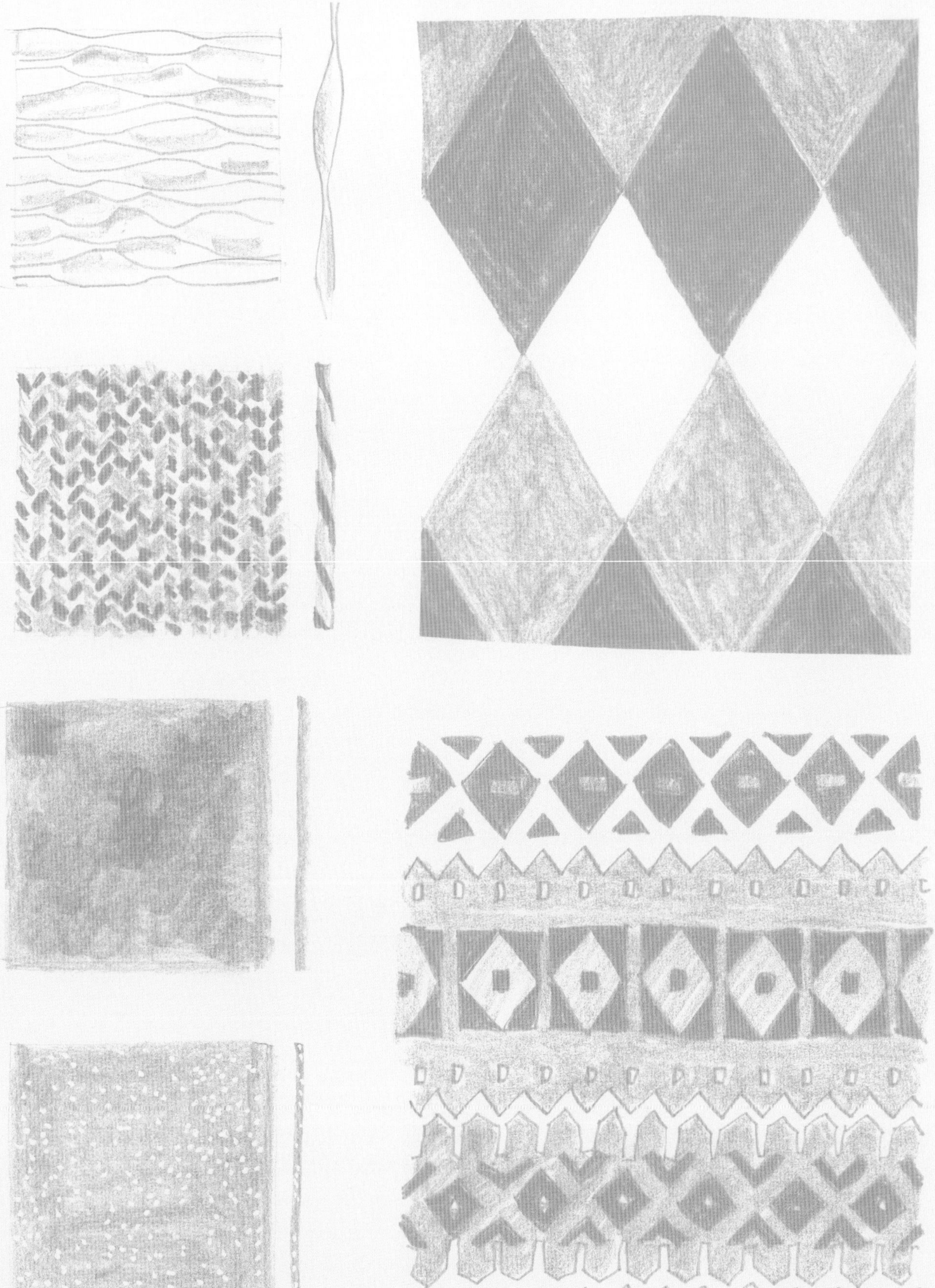

Patterns

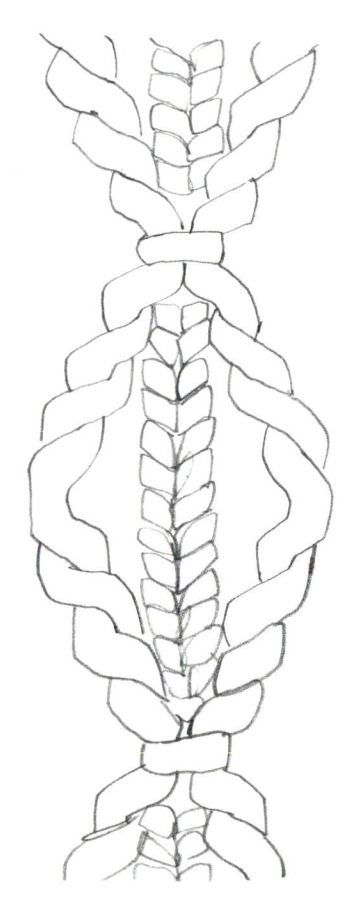

Aran stitch

Drawnwork stitch

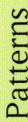

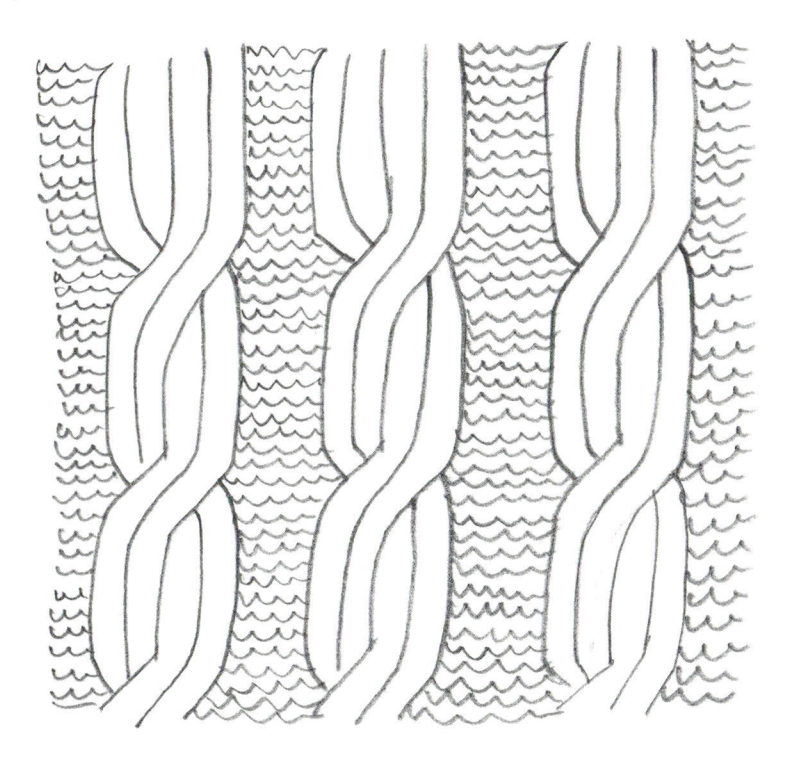

4 needles braid stitch

Cable stitch with motif

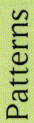

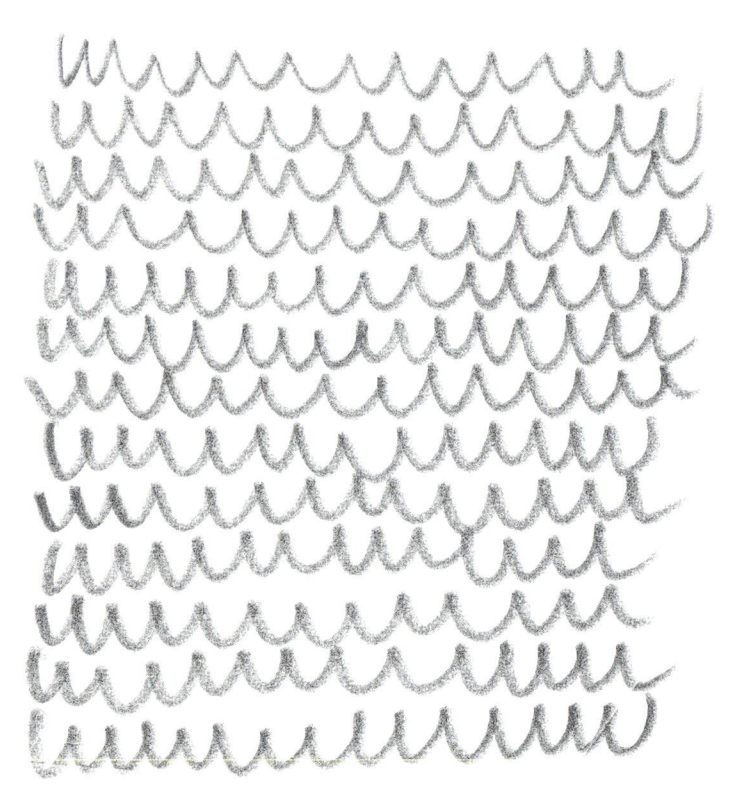

Reverse stitch

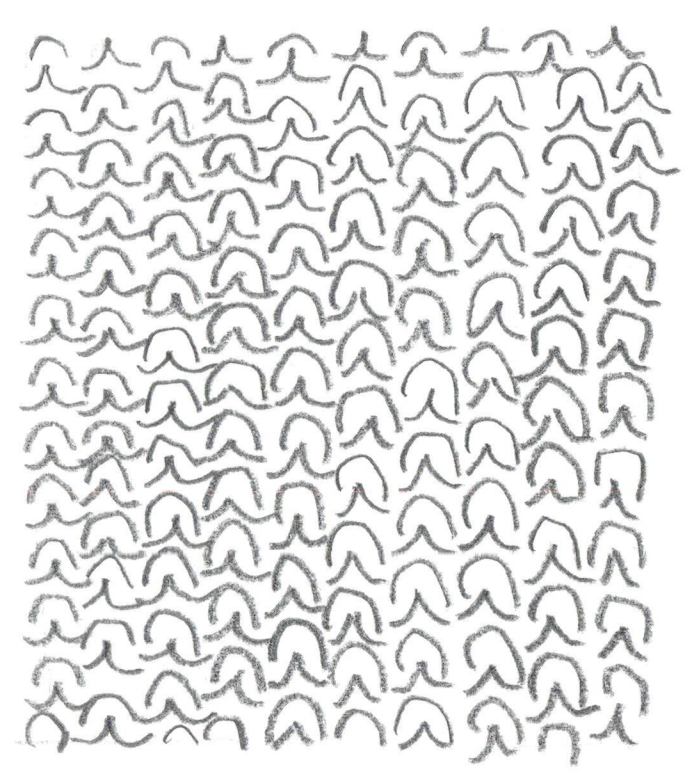

Rice stitch

Patterns

172

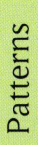

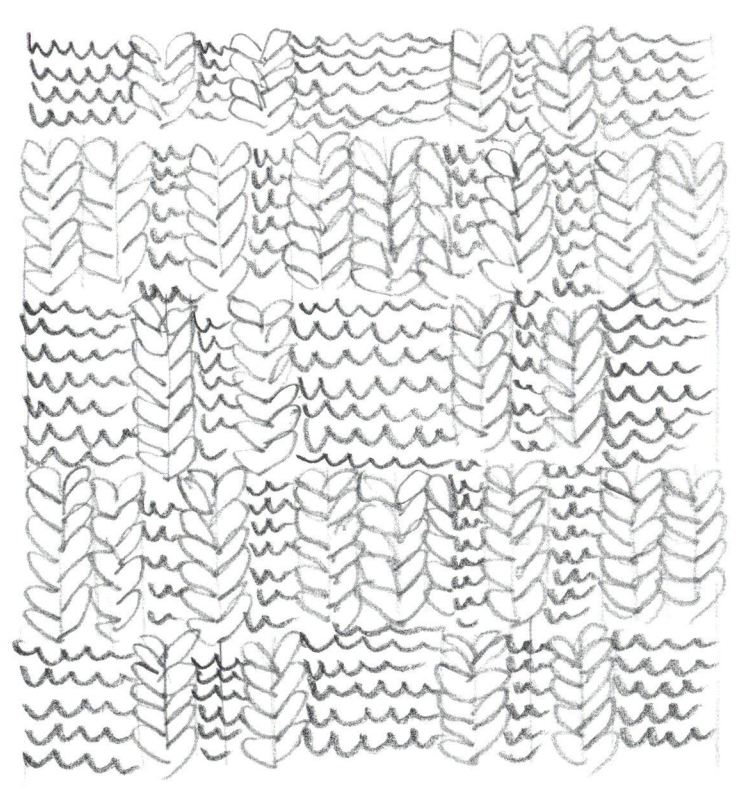

Link stitch (inside/out)

Plain stitch

Patterns

Slubbed yarn

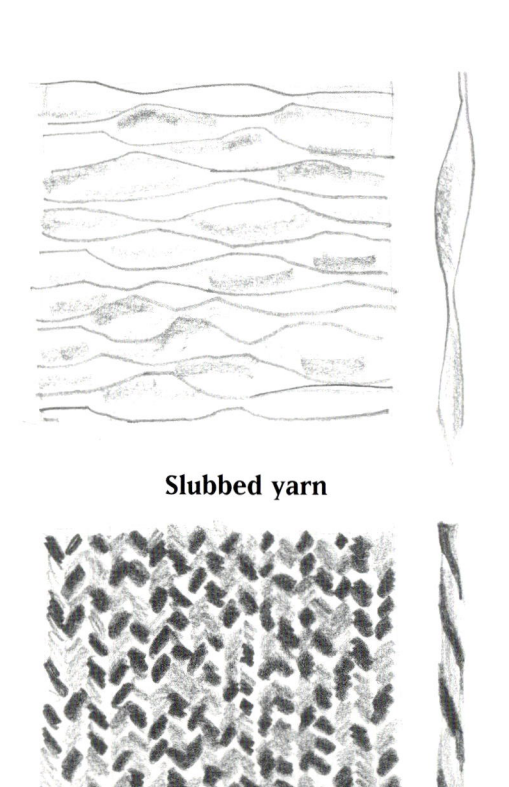

Two-color twist yarn

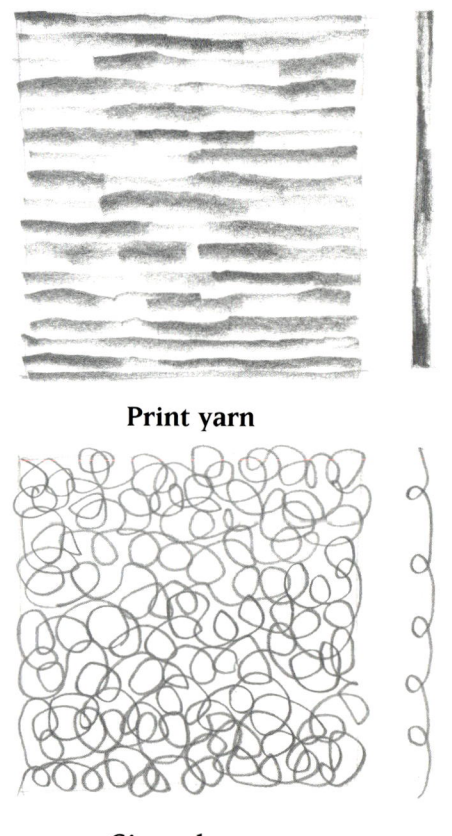

Print yarn

Gimped yarn

Patterns

Mix yarn

Yarn with glitter

Mohair yarn

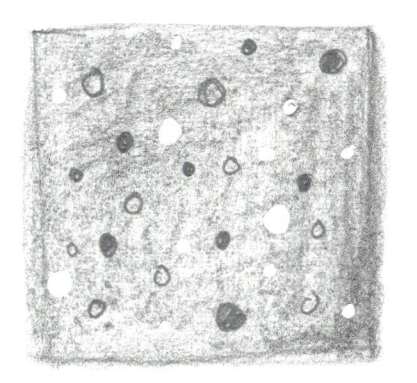

Tweed yarn

Patterns

Cable stitch

Bourrelet stitch

Patterns

Plangui print

Ikat print

Patterns

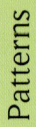

Argyll tarsia yarn

Madras check print

Patterns

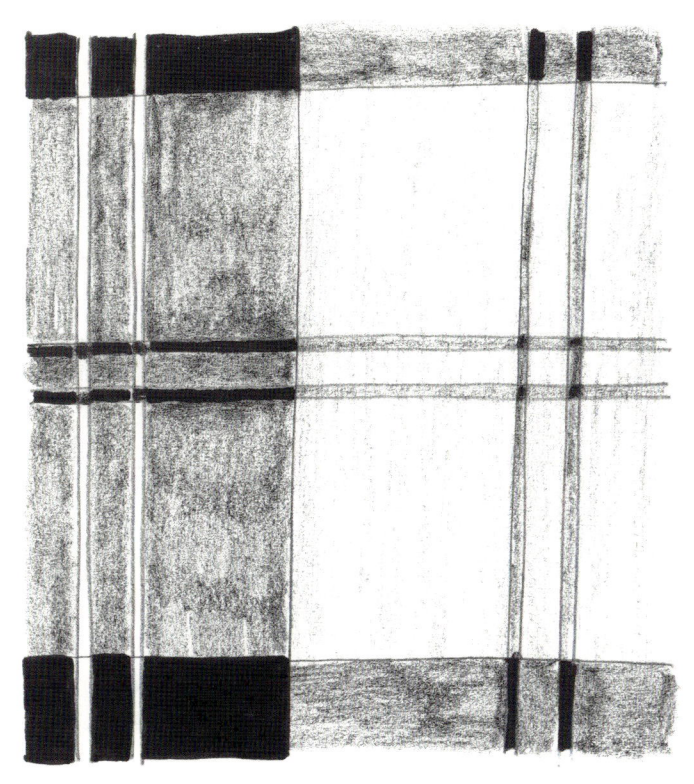

District check print

Jacquard print

Patterns

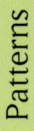

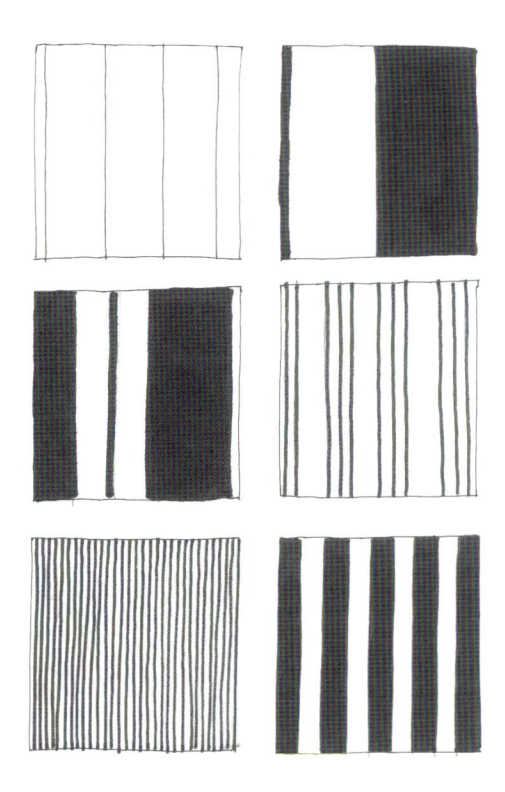

Stripes print

1960s style geometric print

Checkerboard print   **Window print**

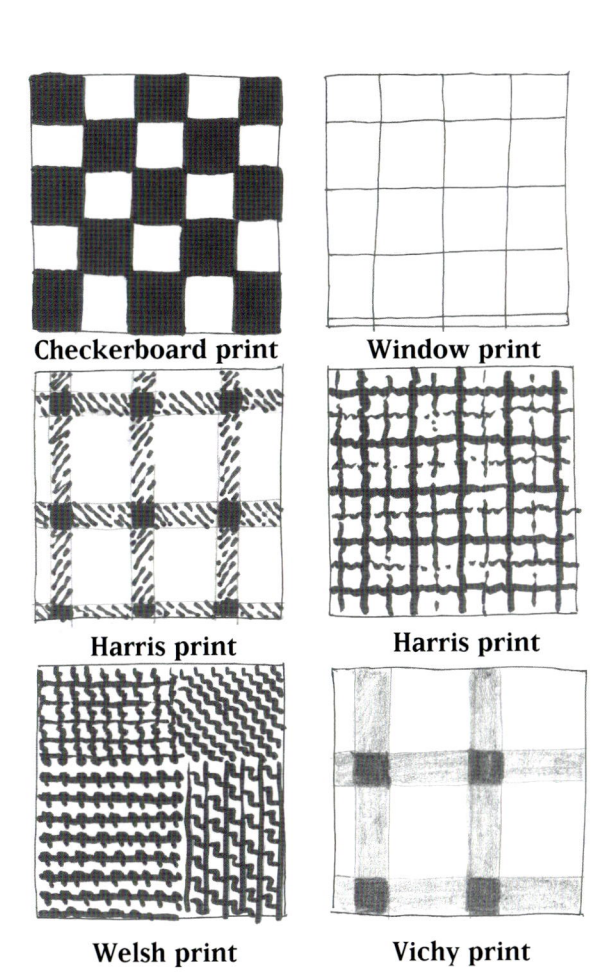

Harris print   **Harris print**

Welsh print   **Vichy print**

Houndstooth print

Patterns

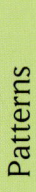

Mackintosh print

Marimekko print

Patterns

182

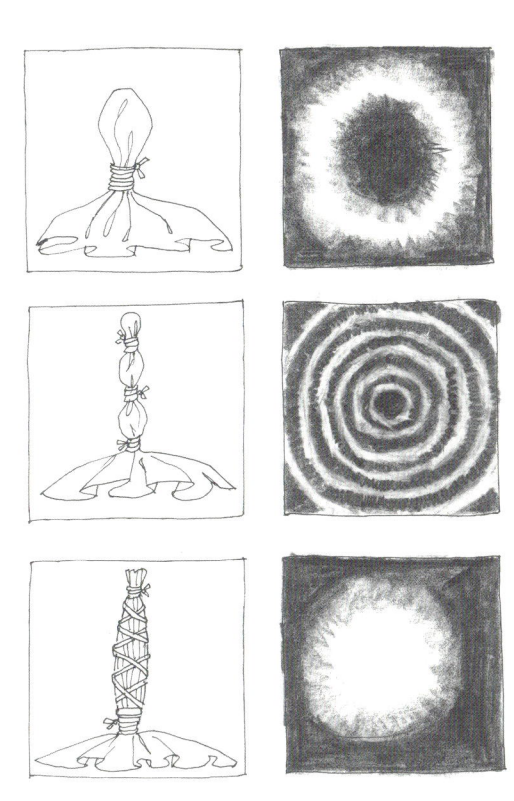

African batik print

African print

Patterns

Art Deco print

Navajo print

Patterns

184

Batik print

Art Nouveau print

Patterns

185

Indian print

Persian print

Patterns

186

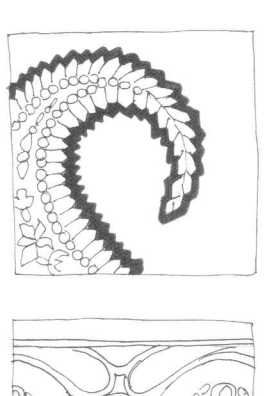

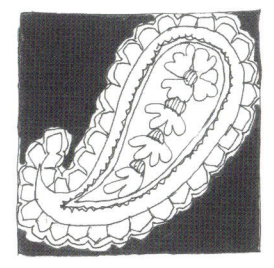

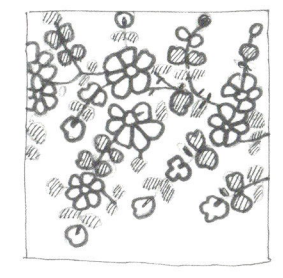

Paisley print

Hawaiian print

Patterns

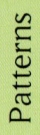

1950s style flower print

1960s style flower print

Patterns

188

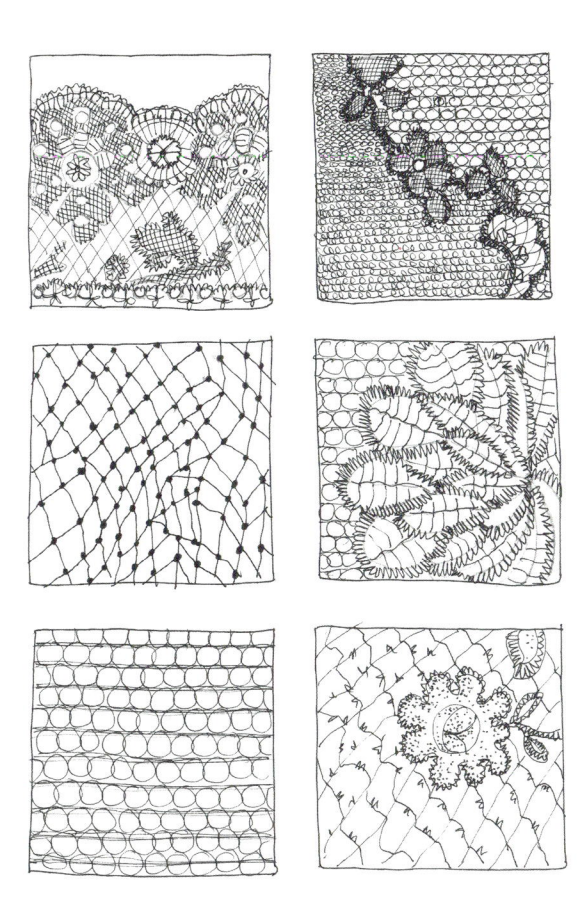

Lace and lace-edging

William Morris print

Patterns

Russian print

Chinese print

Patterns

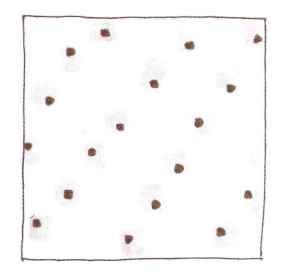

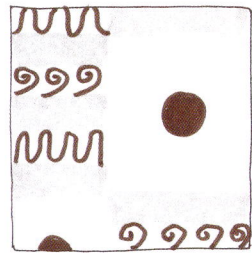

1950s style geometric print

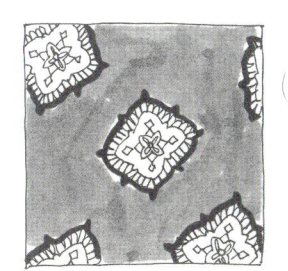

Tie print

Patterns